LIVE IT FULLY. ENJOY!

LIVE IT FULLY. ENJOY!

Everything (is) about Life

Chandrashekar V N

PARTRIDGE

A Penguin Random House Company

To order additional copies of this book, contact
Partridge India
000 800 10062 62
orders.india@partridgepublishing.com

www.partridgepublishing.com/india

Dedicated To:

LIFE

To all that was once alive
To all that is today alive
To all that will one day be alive
To all that which had a chance to live

To all men and women who were once living
To all men and women who are today living
To all men and women who will be one day living
To all who has the gift of being Human Being

PREFACE

LIFE! What a beautiful thing this Life is! What a wonderful thing this life is! It is more beautiful because it has happened to you and me. It is wonderful to have happened to us otherwise how would we see its beauty and wonder, otherwise what would you be and what would I be. No one knows. What a mystery?! Life is a mystery and I have tried to look at it, observe it and understand it all these years of my life in my own way and have tried to record some of those observations in this book.

What is life? I believe that this is an eternal question which has innumerable answers.

This might be one of the most asked questions ever on earth. The eternal question. And for it there are so many answers. I too have many answers and yet I have no answer. I have found that the answer is "for each his own". For you, it is upto you to figure it out for yourself.

Life is a gift. And my life is my highest gift. Life is the highest gift that I have received and that I could ever receive. Life is the best gift given to all. Life is the best gift giver to all. Life is the best gift giver of all because it gives you to you, it gives you all that you need, it gives you all that you seek and it has given you that you didn't even seek. Your Life! Yes, your life. You didn't even ask for it, did you?

Life is like a huge mathematical machine, a mathematical equation. It keeps adding, subtracting, multiplying and dividing. And no more complex stuff. It's all basic mathematics. It's upto you what you want to add to your life, what you want to subtract from your life, what you want to multiply in your life and what you want to divide from life. All that you wish, will and do, will happen. The gist of the whole life lies in knowing what to add, what to subtract, what to multiply and what to divide. That is where lies the genius of a man who has understood the true meaning of life. You could choose to add some virtues or vices. You could choose to subtract some friends or foes. You could choose to multiply joy or sorrow. You could choose to divide pain or happiness.

It's upto you to decide. It's upto you to choose. Life has given you the choice to decide some things in your life. And that some things are many a times the most important things in your life. So decide, calculatedly like a mathematician what you choose. Though you didn't have a choice to choose your life, to start with, you have all the choice to lead one to a large extent on your terms. You have all the choice to make one. A better one. A beautiful one. A principled one on your own terms.

Men often express astonishment over their own achievement. That is because they do not know their own true potential. We don't know our potential. We have all the potential to get all that we need, all that we want. Life can give you all that you could get. Life can give you all that you wish to get. Life can give you all that you will to get. The question is how much you want to get. The question is what you want to get. The question is how you want to get. The question is why you want to get what you want to get. And the answers for all these are within you. YOU. Your life.

And finally what is that you give to the life? What is that you do with it? What is it that you give back to the life? Yes, you could give back to it. You could only give back to it and not take anything out of it. Though it seems like we are constantly taking out of it, getting out of it, we are getting only what we are giving to it. The more you give, the more you get. The better you give, the better you get.

You could give an identity to your life. You could give pride to life that you lived a dignified one. You could give prestige to life that you lived a purposeful one. You could give meaning to life by leading a principled one.

The greatness of life lies not in as much as you can get but in as much as you can give. The more you can give to the life of yours and more so to the life of others the better you will have utilized your life and time. Your life would have achieved something significant, your life would leave behind a legacy, your life would have altered the lives of many for the good, your life would have affected many lives permanently, and your life would have played an important role in the history of the mankind.

You could leave behind a trace to prove that you as you had existed. You could leave behind a legacy to prove that you as you had lived. Some trace that marks your presence. Some trace that you actually had a worthy life. Some trace that lives even after you are long gone as a proof of your existence. It's upto you how you choose to do that. You might invent something new. You might create something great. You might even do something simple which might help one or two. You might choose to change a nation which might help millions. Again its upto you. Whatever it is choose wisely and do it. The beauty of human life is that each individual is bestowed with special gifts, atleast one. Each human being is unique. Find out what you are good at, what your uniqueness is and make best use of it. Show the best of yourself to the world and leave a mark behind. And I only hope that this book will be of a little help to you in that direction.

In this tiny book, compared to the vastness of life, on life, I have in my very limited knowledge and understanding of Life, tried to explore the meaning of Life. I have tried to explore what does this all means to me. What does life mean? During this exploration, I have understood that there are innumerable meanings to life. I have understood that life means nothing and everything and all that is in between.

Life is the epitome of duality. Life is a coin with two faces. Life is both true and false. Life is nothing and everything. Life is zero and infinite. Life is life and death. Life is right and wrong. Life is beauty and beast. Life is a comedy and tragedy. Life is a problem and solution. Life is a truth and a lie. Life is the most simple and most complex thing in the world.

Life is a container and it contains everything. Life has billion different faces. Life has billion different phases. Life has billion different names. Life has billion different frames. Life has billion different forms. Life has billion different norms.

Life is equal to all, life is impartial in the sense that every life has many phases of ups and downs irrespective of our caste, creed, gender, race, religion, region and it ends with death for all. No exceptions whatsoever.

We came from nothing with nothing. We go into nothing. We take nothing. We have nothing to lose. We have nothing to gain. All we get is to see this life, taste this life, experience this life, feel this life, live this life and enjoy this life.

This book has two sections. The first section has, to a large extent, quatrains on life in the "Play your role, Life is a stage" format. The second section has poems of various length on various random topics related to Life.

I know some of the things here in this book sound serious and some sincere. Some silly and some stupid. Some joyous and some jovial. Some dumber and some slumber. Some happy and some sad. Some serene and some irritating. Some trying hard to rhyme and some hitting best to chime. Some longing for enlightenment and some soothing entertainment. Some ignorant and some arrogant. Some innocent and some opinionated. Some childish and some childlike.

You may not like some of these. Best thing you could do is to ignore them and move on to the next. Someone else might like them.

You can smile at my serenity or laugh at my stupidity. I will only be happy for the reason that I was the reason for someone's happiness. You can be concerned with me when I am concerned or condemning the faulty when I am condemning. I will only be glad that I could share my thoughts with you. Let's strive towards making this world a better world. Let's work together to Live this life fully and enjoy it thoroughly.

I have thoroughly enjoyed this journey of Life so far, both my life and my writing of this Life. I am very glad that you chose to join me in this journey. I hope you will enjoy it too. Both this book called Life and your Life.

Life is everything. Everything is life.

LIVE IT FULLY.ENJOY!

Bangalore   Chandrashekar V N
27-10-2015

ANNOUNCEMENT

Dear Friend, I have an announcement to make
I started writing for my own sake
Will write from heart, not any fake
Only a hobby, nothing to give or take
All my life's learning will put and bake
Hope this pastime will help me slake
Will fight for it and see what it can make
Hope it reveals the truth, keep me wide awake
I hope no external thing will put a brake
I know it's not easy and not my cup of cake
I know it's a long chase, a lifelong lake
But then nothing to lose, nothing at stake
I hope this will help my false beliefs shake
I know this will make the false ground, I might be on, quake
I know this is something that I need to carefully undertake
I am glad that I decided in this endeavor to partake
I am sure this never was or will ever be a mistake
I welcome you to heart fully partake
I request you to forgive if there is any mistake
I welcome you to make all that you can make
I welcome you to take all that you can take

Part One

Life is a Journey!

This sections contains quatrains on Life. They try to find an answer to the eternal question "What is Life?". Majority of this quatrains are incomplete in the sense that they could be extended and elaborated even further. I would like to think and believe that all this quatrains together form a long song on Life. They are not arranged in any specific order. I would suggest reader not to rush through the entire content in one sitting or a stretch. Also, I would like the idea of reading one or two stanzas randomly whenever the reader feels down or feels like reading it. I hope the reader enjoys this Journey!

E njoy it, Life is a journey
   That is the secret, that is the key
Nothing else outside this for thee
Traverse your way joyfully and join the sea

Know your place, Life is a race
Keep your peace and maintain your pace
Sure enough success will embrace
Receive your rewards with dignity and grace

Take it seriously, Life is a joke
Often it doesn't go by what it spoke
Use your mind and heart to laugh invoke
Understand its intent and don't go broke

Confront it, Life is a tragedy
Events upon events, determined to test
Do as much as you could to make it a comedy
Face and fight, to the world show your best

Hold it carefully, Life is a container
It contains everything, every ounce
Maintain it perfectly, you are its maintainer
For you only get to live only once

Marvel it, Life is a mystery
Can't be deciphered, even after reading entire history
For everyone's and every day is a new story
Delving too much on it leads only to hystery*

---

*   Hystery – used to rhyme – to mean hysteria

Life is music! To its tunes learn to dance
Be attentive and alert, never get into trance
Learn the beats, with music make romance
Show your best steps for you only get one chance

Play it safe, Life is a game
Never run behind glory and fame
Control your moves, your desires tame
Attain your best and retain a good name

Try and solve it, Life is a problem
It's there for all, there is none without one
It spares none, there never was one without one
It cares none, there never will be one without one
But then, it's only a disguise, its possibilities emblem
Knock all doors, come out with a solution, there's always one

Read through it, Life is a book
There is a lesson in each page, if you carefully look
It only matters what you learn and what you shook
It doesn't matter what you gave or what you took

Steer carefully, Life is traffic
Some ahead, some behind, like a rat race
Maneuver mindfully and maintain your pace
Enjoy your ride, make your travel terrific

Perform with poise, Life is a theatre
No replay, no rehearsal, all time live stage
Understand and anticipate, plunge into the venture
Success of the show depends on how deep you engage

Behold its spell, Life is a magic
It makes something out of nothing
It moves to nothing from something
If you know what it means, it never is tragic

Look at its depth, Life is a river
It flows and falls, with no proper direction
You have to set it right for you are its driver
Steer it towards the ocean with all correction

Take it fully, Life is a chance
You never knew you will be you
Now you are you, but only once
Prove to the world who are you!

Watch out, Life is a game of cricket
Each one has come here to watch with a ticket
Bat your best, throw yourself out of the thicket
Hit a century, before you lose your wicket!

Wonder at it, Life is a miracle
Do you know how it happened to you?
Do you know why it happened to you?
Resort always to the right! Reach its pinnacle!

Choose wisely, Life is a choice
Listen carefully to your inner voice
Follow the right and cut all the noise
There will never be regret but only rejoice!

Weigh yourself, Life is a scale
Balances by loving you as much as you love
Balances by giving you as much as you give
By loving and giving new heights you could scale

Watch yourself, Life is a mirror
Looking at your inner self, you should never terror
Throws back at you each of your faults and error
Watchfully catch and correct your faults, it never is horror

Enjoy the views, Life is a fair
Many coming and many going, you better be fair
Be modest, let your life never be vanity fair
Life and you are a pair, make it a sincere affair

Savor the sweet, Life is a chocolate
Only those who are right, receive its sweetness
Only those who arrive on time, taste its freshness
Enjoy its fullness by being punctual, never be late!

Grow it well, Life is a tree
For those who seek, it never denies its shade
Equally for all, never considering their grade
Care for it well and be tension free

Come out to the sun, Life is light
For those who see, it's a grand sight
Throwing itself on everyone, equally bright
Kill your dark side, you will always be right

Face it with a smile, Life is a camera
Capture the moments, in memories sort and store
Compare yourself, who you were and who you are
With flashes of right light move on to new era

Listen to its lessons, Life is a teacher
Teaches until you learn, not just a preacher
You are always a student under its feet
So much to live, so learn lessons neat

Live carefully, Life is a hell
For those who cheat and lies tell
Peace of mind not even for a spell
All bads ends you up in a deep well

Hold on to it, Life is a hope
For those who sincerely seek, it never says nope
Only thing you need to do is persist and cope
You could climb all mountains with hope's tiny rope

Withstand the sun with will, Life is a desert
Burning sun and boiling sand, its test basis
Face them and thoroughly search, you sure will find oasis
And then you could eat your stomach full of dessert!

Be alert and attentive, Life is an influence
It's going to tempt you to bad, treat you to good
It all depends on what you choose and your mood
The right choice will sure lead you to affluence

Consider carefully, Life is a market
Each one selling things both good and bad
Buy only good and reject all bad
Sell your good and rewards pocket

Take better prevention, Life is a disease
Clear insight could avoid accidents and pain decrease
Better foresight could prevent disasters and peace increase
With all these in place, you could live with more ease

Beware of it, Life is a lie
It attracts and deceives showing a sweet pie
Assess and then accept, better know where you lie
Be sure that you lived truthfully before you die

Accept it, Life is a truth
Strikes upon you without any ruth
It doesn't matter if you know it or not
It shows itself, denying it, you never cannot

Aim perfectly, Life is a dart
Practice and persevere till you learn the art
Try as many times and never ever quit
Until, the bull's eye, you precisely hit

Sell seriously, Life is a business
You are here to make best of yourself and sell
And see that in the market you do well
To sell well you dwell well on your wellness

Be impressed, Life is a impression
Others' on you, your's on others
The gist of it all is your expression
Do it well and wear the cap with feathers

Learn carefully, Life is a school
Tries and teaches you how to be cool
Better to have strong foundation right in young age
Later you could build as much as you could engage

Watch its beauty, Life is a flower
Sharing with you its décor and fragrance
Giving you a chance, to its beauty experience
What you do with it depends on your clever

Find the pattern, Life is random
Watch closely this chaotic kingdom
In the randomness lies its beauty
To find that for you is your duty

Play your role, Life is a stage
On which all of us are actors
All are equally important factors
What matters is how well you engage

Fill it well, Life is a page
To begin with it is all blank
But leave it with your story, like a sage
So that others can use it as a bank

Take it well, Life is a picture
It's there for you all that you can capture
In your take you be a perfection monger
So that your image lasts longer

Watch it fully, Life is a cinema
Grasp the theme for it's an enigma
Direct it right to sit back and relax
Lead it well to have a better climax

Read it well, Life is an epic
Of kidnaps and crimes, of wars and battles
Its message and magnitude surely baffles
Learn from it, it's written on every relic

Use it well, Life is a magic-wand
Its moves are very difficult to understand
With a slight move it can change the land
Make sure to take its charge into your hand

Choose your side, Life is a fence
The other side might look green, use your prudence
To be on the right side, use your confidence
Be in your limits and never make an offence

Face it well, Life is an encounter
Of facts and by fiction, of truth and by lies
Of the hunted and the hunter
One must counter all these before one dies

Keep it safe, Life is gold
So pure, so shining, its glory can't be told
Glitters still, as it gets old, even in the mist
Be like that, become an alchemist

Create one, Life is a trend
Follow it along all its curves and bend
Create a new one well before your end
Your own self it must transcend

Love all, Life is love
The more you show, the more it grows
It's the greatest emotion that man knows
The purest one as white as dove

Be selective, Life is an attraction
It pulls you towards the things
It promises to give you wings
Maintain attention, don't heed to distraction

Do it well, Life is a job
Do it but without any reserve
What you do decides what you deserve
Don't just be one among the mob

Find your place, Life is a musical-chair
Fantastic and fun filled game, but there is always one less
You can't have everything, there will be many that you miss
Get along with what you have like in a musical choir

Be strong, Life is a chain
It's as strong as its weakest link
It can break just in an eyes blink
Get stronger and reduce the pain

Follow it well, Life is a trend
With its own ways it changes and amends
For those who want to follow, request it sends
Know its ways and make it a friend

Have fun, Life is a party
Give place for others, be flexible and not sappy
Don't spoil the fun, don't make it dirty
Everyone is there to make merry and be happy

Take it easy, Life is a cinch
If only you take it inch by inch
You would be happy you could easily clinch
You might not believe, you might need a pinch!

Choose your court, Life is a shuttle
Going from this to that, here and there
Moving constantly from somewhere to nowhere
Moving constantly from nowhere to somewhere
Explore everything everywhere before you finally settle

Choose your books, Life is a library
Stacked in it are all sorts of works and books
Next to each other that which are contrary
One gets to see for what one looks

Be spellbound, Life is divine
It intoxicates you without wine
You will be lost but then you will be fine
What all can happen with it you cannot divine

Keep it safe, Life is a treasure
Store it well, take correct measure
Know it's worth and have the pleasure
Use it well and remove all pressure

Know the unknown, Life is a voyage
From known to the unknown
An eternal task you have to own
Reach your destination before you age

Be strong, Life is tuff
Yes, it's not an easy stuff
Around it you cannot bluff
For it's a steep strong cliff

Select your subject, Life is a book
Covering everything of every subject
Containing everything and every object
You could get for what you would look

Be involved, Life is a feat
Achieve it, attain it with all your meat
Work for it and don't accept defeat
Having reached, keep grounded, your feet

Choose the right one, Life is a product
In its different forms it will seduct
Many different choices, your time fast deduct
But choose the right one by your right conduct

Be rightful, Life is a right
One has it since birth to death
Exert it to do only the right
So that it lasts even after your death

Win it, Life is a fight
Between the meek and the might
Between the wrong and the right
To win it you need the right insight

Do right screening, Life is a screen
Project on it all that you can
It will take in everything it can
For it has space and time umpteen

Be involved, Life is a partnership
Among family and relatives, a perfect relationship
Among friends and colleagues, a true companionship
To make and maintain use your craftsmanship

Play your role, Life is a curtain
Your play is only until it falls
After its fall everything stalls
Finish your play well before, be certain

Keep moving on, Life is a marathon
A long one with destination unknown
You move on based on what is already known
Keep crossing whatever you bump upon

Put it on, Life is an ornament
Decorate yourself with it on your neck
Or decide to hide it in a remote deck
And later for not using it please don't lament

Be daring, Life is a nightmare
To those who know not how to dare
For every problem a solution is there
Maybe we are just not aware

Be fair, Life is unfair
Pushes problems on you that you cannot bear
Do your best, be patient and always be fair
The seeds you have sown will sure fruits bear

Decide well, Life is a decision
For what you decide is what you do
And what you become is decided by what you do
Hence make them all with perfect precision

Mix well, Life is a union
A multitude of things, same and opposite
A mixture of things, simple and composite
Be a right part of this sacred communion

Be prepared, Life is a hurricane
Whence it comes whither it goes
What it does, no one knows
Be ready to take the beatings from its cane

Know its reach, Life is infinite
It's very vast, space and time are its limits
You are just a point in it, know your limits
For you are very minute, you are very finite

Know the flow, Life is a pendulum
Move with it, swing your head and hum
Moving between extremes to and fro
It's in these moves that we all grow

Know its roots, Life is diverse
It's as vast as this universe
We cannot capture it in a verse
That which is so short and terse

Move along, Life is a progression
From childhood to adulthood
From cradle to death bed
Go on well with it without transgression

Create your fate, Life is an estate
Its boundaries no one can estimate
Its reach you can't guess at any rate
But make sure to maintain it in better state

Face it right, Life is a catastrophe
Maintain it well, face it with a genuine smile
Manage it well, your message goes a long mile
And at the end win the life time trophy

Do it well, Life is a task
Do it openly without any mask
Do it such that no one can ask
Do it so that in its glory you may bask

Rise high, Life is a ladder
Rise up to reach its top
Be confident and be bolder
Until you reach you never stop

Move along, Life is a wind
Pushing hard on you when it's blind
Gently swaying on you when it's kind
That's its way, you better know its mind

Be courageous, Life is a cage
Boundaries on all sides, you are not going to go out alive
So, live it fully when you still have a chance to live
To lead one of your own, all you need is courage

Know its flow, Life is a lake
Flowing constantly taking all that comes along
Until it reaches its destiny, distance so long
All along its flow you must be wide awake

Make it clear, Life is an image
Sometimes clear and sometimes hazy
Strive to keep it clear, don't be lazy
So your name remains ages after your age

Write it well, Life is a novel
Of tales and twists, of facts and fiction
Of words and wit, of dialect and diction
With all your will make yours novel

Go fishing, Life is a pond
Know the tricks and knacks to do your fishing
Get along well with fellow fishers, have right bond
And at the end, give a better finishing

Beat it, Life is like weather
Most studied but still unpredictable
When unpleasant becomes unbearable
When pleasant you don't have to bother

Be ready always, Life is change
All throughout, that is the only constant
You can't know its reach and range
Which can take turn just any instant

Choose yours, Life is a square
Four classes and four sides
Four ends and four modes
Which one to be in and when, be aware!

[Four classes – Brahmana, Kshatriya, Vaisya and Shudra
      Brahmana – The intellect or the one who is involved with
the work of brain for living
      Kshatriya – The Warrior or the one who protects for living
      Vaisya – The businessman or the one who does business
for living
      Shudra – The worker or the one who depends on physical
labor for living

Four Sides – Brahmacharya, Grihastha, Vaanaprastha and
Sanyasa
      Brahmacharya - Student Stage
      Grihastha - Householder Stage
      Vaanaprastha - Hermit Stage
      Sanyasa - Wandering Ascetic Stage

Four Ends – Dharma, Artha, Kama and Moksha
      Dharma: Righteousness, Duty
      Artha: Wealth
      Kama: Desire
      Moksha: Liberation

Four Modes – Saama, Daana, Bheda and Danda
      Saama: placation
      Daana: presentation
      Bheda: partition
      Danda: persecution]

Spot the gold, Life is a mine
It could either be bomb or gold
Spotting it or making it is in your hold
It's their in everyone's, yours and mine

Be strong willed, Life is will
You will be what you will to be
For you can be what you will to be
Leave a blank check for all, your final will

Know it right, Life is immortal
Breathed by the mother earth and nature
They will continue to exist, though we are mortal
They will know it those who are mature

Try and tame, Life is wild
At times free and furious, it's untamable
At times forms innumerable, it's unnamable
Know its nature, be Nature's own child

Plan it well, Life is a grand-plan
It takes its own course while you are busy planning
To the world of reality, it wakes you up canning
Try and belong to the "expect the unexpected" clan

Know the tunes, Life is a raga
Enchanting variations at all times
Beautiful, melodious musical tunes
Be a bright part of this never ending saga

Place well, Life is an order
When you are right, you give it out
When you are wrong, you take it out
Giving and taking, always on border

Serve yourself, Life is a buffet
Serving all sorts of exquisite dishes
Each one could fulfill all that he wishes
Be careful in choosing, so it would not buffet

Don't be tempted, Life is a temptation
Tempts through all sorts of things full of competition
But you stick to your ground and stand firm
To your own principles, you always affirm

Be a rightful judge, Life is a court
Face the truth, every day is a judgment day
And the outcome depends on what you court
For being right, every day is a right day

Know its use, Life is an instrument
You can use it to create music or movement
What you use it for and how, is up to you
For the owner and user of it is only you

Direct it, Life is a wind
You can, for the control is in mind
Assess and don't simply follow blind
Ascertain and follow only the kind

Do well, Life is a service
Selfless one averts every vice
To do best possible, you are your device
To do your best, you must, a method device

Wear it well, Life is a crown
You could be ascended to the power of throne
In its glory careful not to drown
Do your best and never be a drone

Be alert and attentive, Life is an inspection
Of the world around and all its product
And the highest of all is the introspection
Of your thoughts, words, deeds and conduct

Give its shape, Life is water
It takes the shape of its container
Give yours for you are its maintainer
Do it soon and do not regret later

Decorate it well, Life is a sculpture
Create your masterpiece, you are its sculptor
Its shape comes from your taste and culture
Make it the centerpiece, place it on a high altar

Make it right, Life is an appointment
Never miss it, not even a moment
For having missed you will later lament
Missed is lost, only a disappointment

Play it well, Life is a ball
For every throw that you throw
It comes back to you and grow
You better be a strong supporting wall

Build it strong, Life is a hive
Build it by being as busy as a bee
Build it right so you could peacefully live
For all your efforts you could be glee

Feel it in full, Life is a kiss
That you would never want to miss
Be prepared for everything it brings with open lips
Yeah that's a smile! And I can give no more tips

Go with it, Life is a flight
Struggle hard and give a strong fight
Take it from wrong to right
Only then will you see the true light

Be keen, Life is a discovery
Of its secrets, its glory and mystery
You are in charge of its full recovery
Enjoy the ride and join the books of history

Maintain it clean, Life is a matter
Of serious note and so don't clutter
With all unwanted junk and litter
For it's the highest matter made out of matter
For it's the highest matter that matter

Be inspired, Life is a spark
Ignited with imagination, burns like wildfire
Act on your dreams and create a mark
With reminiscences of achievement, peacefully retire

Light it right, Life is a candle
Burn it to brighten up a dark room
Or use it to burn up the whole room
Make sure which one you want to handle

Keep your poise, Life is a see-saw
Merryful play of going up and down
There is joy in every trip that you didn't foresaw
Enjoy the ride even while you are going down

Paint well, Life is a painting
You are the canvas, you are the painter
Don't leave a black mark, not even a single tainting
Paint it perfect and clear, not fainter

Draw it well, Life is a drawing
Draw it as you would love to be, drive it and then live to be
From your account, everyday it's withdrawing
Before being out, be what you always wanted to be

Be sportive, Life is a sport
Peaceful participation is more import
Play all that you want, win all that you will
Learn all the good deeds and earn all the goodwill

Tender with care, Life is a grove
Decide what you want to grow
Plant all the seeds in a perfect row
Enjoy the fruits before you go to grave

Keep it clean, Life is an account
And you are its sole holder
Keep it transparent and be bolder
Then you need not worry on any count

Give the right angle, Life is a triangle
Of past, present and future
Of yours, others and nature
See that all is well from all angle

Follow with force, Life is a mission
Endeavor enthusiastically until you attain
Escaping all false traps without submission
At the end, your name and fame, you will retain

Be prepared, Life is a storm
Taking you by surprise by its force
It's not unusual and it's not even norm
For on it there is no such rule to enforce

Be conscious, Life is a rumbling
Working constantly beneath and behind
Can shatter down all dreams in one tumbling
Or can calm down for a peaceful mankind

Keep fighting, Life is boxing
With all the strength that you can muster
Give it a strong blow, be your own master
Come out a winner, without much taxing

Keep keen eyes, Life is an observation
You are the observer and you are the observed
The process should lead you to elevation
Have views and vision, to get mankind served

Know the keys, Life is a lock
The key here is to have the right key
When you know your key, it's turnkey
It works perfect, just like clock

Unveil the veil, Life is a mask
Concealing treasure in the form of a task
Revealing only to those who bother to ask
And then giving pleasure to be able to bask

Give it a shape, Life is a concept
For which there is no set precept
Takes its own form for each one
You shape it for you but no one

Grow up and Grow well, Life is a cradle
Under its influence you are always a child crying
With tiny little steps, reach to all that you can handle
Attain your full potential before you die or die trying

Seek blessings, Life is a temple
Many ideals and many idols, example ample
Worship and follow the right one with respect and reverence
Such that someone later could make your reference

Be watchful, Life is a game of snakes-and-ladders
Sometimes beaten high up to reach the top
Sometimes bitten to bottom down, sudden shudders
From all the rises and falls, keep your mind atop

Be bold and positive, Life is a battlefield
And in that you are the sole warrior
Pitching against yourself all the negative shield
With a strong positive attitude, come out of that barrier

Catch the watch, Life is a hunt
Keen ears and sharp eyes make you a hunter
Sweet smile and soft words, don't ever be blunt
You will have a fine catch, you would be a punter

Build it right, Life is a pyramid
Broader the base, taller could be its height
Stronger the base, it doesn't fall on its weight
With hurricanes all around, you could still stand amid

Be ready, Life is a renovation
Of the old ideas by the new
Initiated and acted by a few
Be renewed and find your salvation

Go play it, Life is a game of hide-and-seek
Keep off from all the bad, always hide
Follow only the right and have a jolly ride
For what you get is what you seek

Write it well, Life is a writing
Of a piece, a poem or a prose
Of all happenings since you rose
Make sure it to be gripping

Keep filling, Life is an hour-glass
Every wasted moment, its sands sinking
Make most out of it by your thinking
You will then belong to a different class

Select well, Life is a collection
Of memories and of moments
Of events and of movements
Be sure you have a better selection

Experience it thoroughly, Life is an experience
Every fleeting moment brings a new one
Only it can surpass it, comparable none
Enjoy it fully for you get it only once

Get attracted, Life is a magnet
Two opposing poles apart, still attracting
You can never escape from its net
The unified dualism, always enticing

Follow it well, Life is a religion
Benefiting all, irrespective of race or region
Be good and do good is its ultimate principle
Follow it through, you will reach its pinnacle

Be firm and strong, Life is a hurricane
With force and pressure without any direction
If by your presence you make correction
It will be sweet, just like sugar from sugarcane

Be choosy, Life is a obsession
For pleasure and power, for name and fame
For all possible material possession
But be warned, it's only a pursuit of shame

Be patient, Life is a wait
For the arrival of an era, a season of light
For the removal of darkness, reason so right
Be constantly moving maintaining the gait

Be adventurous, Life is a exploration
Of gem among men, of minerals in land
Of possibilities in problem to build a strong nation
Don't end up reaching a mirage in sand

Choose yours, Life is a station
Many coming in, many getting out
Many going on, many being left out
Get on to right one, reach your destination

Buy the best, Life is a shop
Everything in it, you could buy or sell
And you will not know its next hop
Before you leave, have all your doubts quell

Find yours, Life is a range
Found in the cycles of decay and growth
Bound in the regions of birth and death
Like a dense forest with constant change

Marvel its magic, Life is a bewitchment
Casting its spell on you, every passing minute
Its magnanimity leaves you in bewilderment
In front of it you are only a dot, how minute!

Handle with care, Life is like balloon
Colorful and full, floating freely
On its own will, treating truly
A pin is enough to kill, careful you buffoon!

Take reign, Life is a realm
Encompassing everything under its domain
Beyond its boundaries nothing remain
You are its centre, have no qualm

Be active, Life is boring
For those who know not what it really is
You can't afford to miss a minute, keep energy soaring
Keep observing and know how beautiful it really is

Be optimistic, Life is like currency
What men attach is what its worth
But you ascertain yours with urgency
And live up to it, happily henceforth

Bet right, Life is a game of dice
It is a fruit of both chance and choice
Make sure for what you want to bet
And take steps and act until you get

Treasure it, Life is like diamond
The more it's cut the more it shines
But today most have taken it to be an almond
And the more one gets the more one whines

Face it with grace, Life is a trial
Your actions and achievements are your jury
Try and get them right without fear or fury
You sure will be acquitted without denial

Be on your mark, Life is a run
From known to the unknown, seen to the unseen
From here to nowhere, been to the unbeen
While on the go, have all the fun

Be well prepared, Life is an audition
For locating the best fine gems among men
Do your best moves, give your best rendition
Try and become one of them, Amen!

Be happy and smiling, Life is a photograph
Always pose to it your picture perfect smiles
They sure will go on strong for long miles
Eternal joy, always an up trending graph

Make your place, Life is a venue
Where all that is, confluence
Where all that can, influence
See what you can, it's the only avenue
Be what you can, that's your best dress
Do what you can, that's your only address

Be proactive, Life is a passage
In time, between the birth and death
On books, through the myths and truth
Keep track of what you pass as you pass age

Be prepared, Life is like rain
You never know when it is going to arrive
Keep your ground prepared with all your drive
It comes on time and soothes all the pain

Pack light, Life is a trip
With baggage full of spins and sins
With luggage full of whims and wins
Move on and merrily end it, and RIP

Find the trend, Life is a cloud
It sure has got its silver lining
Only it needs finding and fine tuning
Then it speaks out, clear and loud

Rule your role, Life is a play
You can choose to play or you will be played with
When you are just a puppet, it's your character slay
Better be a play and be perfect like a goldsmith

Value it right, Life is an asset
The most invaluable, the most precious
The most delicate, better be cautious
It's a league apart, everything belongs to its set

Know your line and hit right on, Life is a missile
Keep on track, train and exercise staunch
Hit right on target, on every single launch
With your success you will be left only to smile

Take charge, Life is a ship
Be its captain, take leadership
Maneuver it right if required with a whip
It follows your whip, a deep friendship

Plan well, Life is a budget
Keep a balanced expense with income
You sure will see a better outcome
That's the best advice a buddy could get

Be prepared to repay, Life is a loan
You will have to repay to it with all interest
Work well to clear its debt, don't groan or moan
You surely will clear if you work with all interest

Be careful, Life is a punch
Be surrounded with the right bunch
Act according to your right hunch
Only then can you have peaceful lunch

Come to terms, Life is a pact
Between you and your inner self
Abide by it and accordingly act
You sure will soon realize your self

Involve your soul, Life is a role
It is accompanied by many a rule
Follow each one with all your whole
You could take its charge and easily rule

Be the king, Life is a ring
Season after season, summer after spring
It never rests in a place, comes back like spring
Be encircled by it, does the bell ring?

Concentrate well, Life is a study
Learn basics right and be steady
It makes you strong and sturdy
To conquer it, you will be ready

Keep practicing, Life is a stunt
Acquire new skills, be on the hunt
Accept all that arrives, never shunt
Do as best you can in your short stint

Read it right, Life is a subject
Study it well and understand its object
Retain only that's required, remaining reject
Spread its secret all around, inspiration inject

Know your scene and act right, Life is an acting
Enriching experience, but then not an easy one though
Takes all your meat and might, tedious and exacting
Once you know the flow, becomes smooth as dough

Explore it well, Life is an exploration
Of opportunities in obstacles like minerals in land
Of possibilities in problems like oasis on sand
Do best to dig them out, to build a strong nation

Seek your semblance, Life is a simile
Its sweet, it's as sweet as a smile
Its short, it's as short as a mile
Keep it short and sweet but not facsimile

Seek your Self, Life is a metaphor
Only it can be compared with itself
All others incomparable to the SELF
They all disappear just like burning camphor

Manage and maintain it well, Life is a database
Of all that will and all that was
Of all that can and all that is
Seek the right samples on which your decisions base

Write the right and write it well, Life is a slate
But many doesn't realize it of late, that one can write it
For they seem to be too busy worried about their future and fate
Realize the reality even if it's a bit late, and write it

Get adjusted, Life is dynamic
Every single minute changes so dramatic
Every single moment fun and fantastic
Spread its joy like a pandemic

Choose your acts, Life is a container
Holds peace and prosperity, has joy and compassion
Unfolds the war and wrath, unveils sorrow and passion
Choose what you want for you are its maintainer

Reach your height, Life is a platform
To launch yourself, to showcase your skill
To do what you tell, to achieve what you will
It only depends on how well you perform

Choose your side, Life is a fight
Of mind over matter, of wrong over right
Of kind over cruel, of meek over might
Choose the right and spread the light

Churn it well, Life is like butter
Silent and subtle, soft and hidden
To see it truly, you need to look better
To know it fully you need your vision widen

See and show well, Life is a showcase
Work well and create a master piece
Make sure to project a strong case
And then you could rest in peace

Be gay and gallant, Life is a gallery
By possessing peaceful word and heart
By portraying pieces of work and art
In it you could be a valuable jewelry

Take a broad view, Life is like iceberg
Beneath its so vast, you see only its tip
To know its depth, take deep dive and dip
And you will see under it a titanic like burg

Choose yours, Life is a drink
Like alcohol, it can show you high and pull you down
If not taken care it can take you to the brink
To be on the safer side make a mix of your own

Remove the wraps, Life is a cocoon
Holding hidden inside a beautiful butterfly
Once it has its wings it will be able to fly
You should too, you better realize it soon

Make right moves, Life is a memoir
A story for others to read, an example for others to follow
A glory for all to celebrate, a savory for others to swallow
Add the right movements and never be a bête-noire

Keep your head high, Life is an expo
A grand one, walk in with an idea
A brand new, talk it out to media
Make sure to manage your tempo

Keep your faith, Life is a tunnel
Light's on the other end, you only need to travel
Use right means, follow proper channel
To meet the bright light at the end and marvel

Bridge the gaps, Life is a channel
To connect the seas, to convey a message
Cover it up right, don't just flannel
Results of which make a perfect passage

Take right action, Life is a result
Of all that is over and the entirety of all of your effort
It should be pleasant, it's ok if you don't own a fort
If it fails to be so, it is its own insult

Keep it straight, Life is a line
Starting on from a strong single locus
Going on in one direction with one focus
It will reach the right end and you will be fine

Be game, Life is a playground
You are here to play, take a round
Play safe and well, don't just fool around
The Supper Cup, at the end will be found

Keep focus, Life is a center
Of everything that is, of everything that will be
What's your target decides what you will be
There is no going back, once you enter

Drive it well, Life is a chariot
Steer it right for you are its charioteer
Take along some others, be a volunteer
Steering it wrong don't take it to warzone
There are others depending on you, you are not alone
Make peace among men, allow not to riot

Look after it well, Life is an antique
You preserve it well and pass on
Take equally both commend and critique
It gets used even after you move on

Keep in the knowing, Life is a tact
Know how to deal, keep it compact
Everything doesn't reveal, learn its impact
Follow the facts and try to be exact

Deliver your best, Life is a tribute
To itself, do all that you can to contribute
Let peace and happiness be your attribute
Go ahead and spread, happily distribute

Find your angle, Life is a triangle
Of thoughts, speech and action
You are always bound in their tangle
Concentrate equally on each fraction

Know your position, Life is a trinity
Of you, your passions and your deity
Of you, your relations and the society
Work with all, the strength is unity

Understand it, Life is a disaster
If only you don't know how to master
Know its nuances, better and faster
Know its reach, make your vision vaster

Do it right, Life is a math
Of right actions addition
Of sweet memories multiplication
Of sins and sorrows division
Of misery and pain's subtraction
Use the right math, create a right path

Know your song, Life is a thesaurus
Takes different meanings, knows no norms
Reaches new limits, invokes different forms
Go on, sing gladly along with the chorus

Get the right one, Life is a post
Receive all well, be a good host
Seal all the matter, store all in the letter
Pass on to the future, hold on to the better

Mange it well, Life is a profession
Maintain policy, discipline and punctuality
For all your mistakes, make a confession
You will obtain peace and popularity

Watch carefully, Life is a spectacle
You are the spectator, you are the seen
To know clearly, to your mind, wear a pure spectacle
You will see what is seen and what is unseen

Play well, Life is a playground
Lots of games like magic merry-go-round
But within its limits you are bound
The way you play, in future shouldn't hound
So be your best and be a player all-around
Rewards of it will be all abound

Check your input, Life is a computer
Be selective about what you see, hear and utter
Reads all the information, takes all the input
Feeds on its logic and magic, pushes out the output

Build it right, Life is a castle
Built on your dreams, built out of your deeds
Build from your heart, Build according to your needs
Give a new form, be an apostle

Sleep well, Life is a bed
Of dreams and despair, of thorns and roses
For a peaceful sleep follow what said Moses
To the right place you will be led

Follow it right, Life is a guide
It has all the rules you just have to abide
It has all the answers, you just have to unhide
Be on the right side, you will have a jolly ride

Be truthful, Life is a safe
Stores your secrets, protects your self
Know the right keys and have relief
Be sinless and you will be safe

Know its mode, Life is a device
You define and design it, be wise
A perfect purpose, you need to device
Be sure to be away from avarice and vice

Be the right one, Life is a drop
In this eternal universe, in this vast ocean
It can create a flood, it can create crop
It can change its state and what it mean
Learn and earn all that you can until you drop

Be involved, Life is a campaign
For a vote, for a right
For a cause, for the light
Be clear about what you champion

String it well, Life is a string
Producing soothing music from the guitar leads
Forming a beautiful necklace out of orphan beads
You design it, you are the master of the ring

Make it vast, Life is a field
Protecting everyone under its shield
To everyone, motherly care does it wield
Make sure you produce maximum yield

Be cheerful, Life is a spirit
Of different persons, of different patterns
So subtle, can't be seen even with lanterns
To mind and to find, have the right spirit

Keep pursuing, Life is a cry
To attain the peace, to reach the sky
To achieve equality, to go miles high
You can have them all, you just have to try

Be prepared, Life is automatic
Doesn't wait for anything or anyone, it goes on
Takes along those who come along, it moves on
While you are on the flow be pragmatic

Keep your count, Life is a counter
Exchange your time coupon and ask for more
For all that it brings, be ready to encounter
Be patient, in less you could see more

Be light hearted, Life is a lightening
It can happen in a second and it can be over too
Its effects far reaching and frightening
But using its light you could learn and earn too

Study it well, Life is a chapter
Covering all studies and subjects
Having all matter and objects
Know it all well before ends your chapter

Be careful, Life is a crime
If not used to its peak when in prime
Make best use of all your time
For its more worth than all your time

Find your place, Life is a conflict
Between heart and mind, between religion and science
Between cruel and kind, between war and peace
Love all and hatred never inflict

Come to terms, Life is a compromise
Between what you get and what you want
Between what you can and what you can't
But make sure not to compromise on your promise

Get on soon, Life is a train
A track to go on, a goal to reach
Why to do, where to go, you have to teach
How to do, what to do, you need to train

Make it good, Life is a stay
A short one, very transient
Make it sweet with work and play
It could be only if you are transparent

Take participation, Life is a sport
It throws strong opponents, to make you stronger
It shows tough events, to make you tougher
Take them all in a good spirit, be a sport

Choose a place, Life is a park
All sorts of people parking, jogging and playing joyfully
Some going, some coming, keeping it occupied fully
At the end, what matters is where you yourself park

Watch selectively, Life is a television
And you have its remote control
You see what you seek, you can patrol
Monitor it carefully to have a clear vision

Be on the right side, Life is a tug-of-war
Peace on one side war on the other
Love on this side hate on the other
You better decide which way to go and how far

Preserve it, Life is a treasure
You will live but only once, how rare
But then you don't seem to care
What you are doing, are you sure?

Write it well, Life is a slate
Write on it what you will, for you hold the chalk
And follow what you write, walk your talk
For that is how you write your fate

Fill it right, Life is a cheque
When it came it was blank and opaque
You could just write only one
Followed by hundred zeroes or none

Use it well, Life is a vehicle
To take you where you want to travel
To show you that you want to marvel
Enjoy the ride and explore the miracle

Savor it, Life is a sweet
You need to know how and what to taste
Without which every sweet is a waste
Just like missing the evening birds tweet

Follow it well, Life is a drama
You never know what happens when
It just happens leaving you wondering what then
To know more, read the story of Rama

Know its routes, Life is a cave
Rotten and hidden inside all that you save
Shows out in glory all that you gave
Know its width and ride on the wave

Come out of monotony, Life is creativity
Do something, be occupied with some activity
New things that you create will sure create new you
Your creations, after you are long gone, must identify you

Try and solve it, Life is a puzzle
Like rain, from where does it drizzle?
Throws at you, a day at a time
Its upto you, how you use your dime!

Enjoy its simplicity, Life is simple
It's only in our mind that it is complex
It's as simple as your smile forming a dimple
Deep inside its million muscles multiplex

Conjoin with it, Life is a competition
Prompts you to chase it, a temptation
If you play with it, you will win the game
Play against it and you will lose, what a shame!

Wage prudently, Life is a war
Your enemies inside you, not too far
Kill them all but yourself not shattered into piece
Come out neat and clean, the ultimate aim is peace

Care carefully, Life is a precious thing
Attracts you to it, by almost anything
But nothing will be yours, learn to be detached
You will become life's child, universally attached

Behold its beauty, Life is beautiful
Enjoy its serenity, reasons plentiful
Flowers on plants, fruits on trees, how colorful
Moon so shy, sun so high, wow wonderful!

Learn fast, Life is an institution
Its own regulations, its own rules
Its own subjects, its own styles
Be sure to know its constitution

Be happy for you have got it, Life is a gift
That's the highest you could get, be thankful for it
Utilize it fully for your own uplift
You only get once, make best use of it

Play well, Life is a card game
The dealing hand is unknown and you can't blame
The best of you will be known when you have worst of cards
Only when you toil in the soil can you happily eat the curds

Try and excel, Life is an art
It's not very easy to be taught
But everything needed is in your heart
It's so very priceless, it can never be bought

Plan and prioritize, Life is a project
Time is the resource, death is the deadline
Its upto you, how you work and project
You will either be sour or always on cloud nine

Be surprised, Life is a surprise
It has happened to us without our knowing
We never asked or never paid any price
But now it's as real as the sun glowing

Savor its sweetness, Life is a jam
Sometimes harsh spite, like in the traffic jam
Sometimes sweet fruit, like in the bread and jam
Learn to enjoy bread and jam even in a traffic jam

Refine and redefine, Life is a process
Your task is to continuously increase its prowess
Then and only then will you make any progress
Otherwise, whatever you do, it will only be a mess

Sow the right seeds, Life is a garden
Water regularly, weed off clearly, you are its warden
If not maintained well, on you it will harden
You have existed and you were just a burden

Dualities everywhere, Life is a coin
Obstacles, failures, problems and the pain
Vision, success, solutions and the gain
All go hand in hand, for there is no gain without pain

Be courageous, Life is cruel
For the deprived, for the depressed
For the down trodden, for the oppressed
Fight for the weak, to differences quell

Play right, Life is a game
Comes in different forms, many name
Play it well to win and gain fame
Don't make wrong moves and fall to shame

Be the change, Life is a transition
From this to that, from here to there
From past to future, from there to nowhere
All the time you better know your position

Beat the heat, Life is fire
Turns to ash those who dare to come near
Shows the light for those who are dear
Know its beauty before you retire

Be the strongest, Life is a chain
Of events and of actions
Of the sun and the rain
Know your acts to get your reactions

Know the truth, Life is a satire
Money is more valued than man
Attitude is less valued than attire
Try and change this as much as you can

Practice the right, Life is a theory
Of relations and of relativity
Of reasons and of reality
Put your best to practice and bring it to glory

Be broad, Life is vast
Limited only by your imagination
Restricted only by your deeds and action
Its upto you, how much you want to walk past

Keep going on, Life is a road
Of twists and turns, keep moving ahead
Of cuts and curves, be always on board
Face all the blocks, keep a high head

Be sacrificing, Life is a candle
Burning itself it lights up the world
Yourself, you better know how to handle
You can really make a better world

Go by rules, Life is law
It's once for all, no amendments, no by-law
Powerful and perfect, not even a single flaw
Know that no one can escape its strong claw

Catch the subtlety, Life is a wave
Of floating water, light and air
Of flowing thoughts we all share
Realize the pleasure all these gave

Be confident, Life is a gale
In front of it you should not look pale
Face it well and make your's a good tale
Work and play so you could fly in laughter gale

Keep growing, Life is a forest
Work towards your goal, never rest
Be diverse, containing nature's best
Try and grow to be the tallest

Know the taste, Life is a feast
Behold the beauty, bury the beast
Enjoy all there is, worry least
You will rise like the sun in the east

Be active, Life is a storm
Hitting you by surprise is its norm
Be alert, always be in form
Face it else you will end up in dorm

Go on well, Life is a path
Your destination depends on the one you chooseth
Explore and unfold what best it hath
Good or bad you will and must face its wrath

Keep it cool, Life is ice
Melts away in moments, very nice
But everyone wants a big slice
For their meal to add spice

Choices and chances, Life is a sequence
Of events and states, of all the choices you make
Of acts and fates, of all the chances you take
And you will have to face all the consequence

Look at its splendor, Life is a rainbow
Its secret source, you don't know
At the end where it goes, you will never know
A perfect wonder, take a bow!

Go forth, Life is a chase
Go behind your dreams until you achieve
Go beyond your strength until you arrive
Go get it, come out of the encase

Take right part, Life is a party
Serve the people, be the right host
Uphold the rules, be the right guest
Enjoy it, have full fun; hearty

Be the programmer, Life is a code
Maintain its format, Write it right
It's hard to decipher, know how to decode
Learn its language and get it right

Go shopping, Life is a mart
Choose the right, be smart
Fill your stuff and pull your cart
You have to prove your heart's art

Be good at it, Life is a bargain
The better you do, the better your gain
Once you do it, you want to do it again
But remember that no pain no gain

Keep track, Life is a count
That's the highest, that's the paramount
Nothing can buy it, whatever amount
Nothing ever can be its tantamount

Keep trying, Life is an ordeal
It's tuff, better learn how to deal
It's difficult, better know how to heal
And every minute of it you must feel

Go figure, Life is a scheme
A grand one in which everything has its place
With perfect co-ordinates of time and space
You better follow that theme

Keep track of it, Life is a record
Be sure to beat yourself every time
Be sure to account for every dime
With your own book attain concord

Reign it right, Life is a empire
With no limits, with no boundaries
But with qualms, but with quandaries
Rule it carefully for you are its umpire

Feel it full, know it well, Life is magnanimous
By its beauty and magnificence you will go numb
By its elegance and enormity you will go dumb
Leave behind your mark, don't go anonymous

Find your role, Life is a soap
Concentrate on character, your soul supreme
Neglect all chatter, narrate only the theme
Else it slips away, like from wet hands, a soap

Know it well, Life is a epic
Vast and enormous, perfectly spic
Cannot be contained in a single pic
Make yours an important topic

Belong to it, Life is a tribe
Its diversity, all words cannot describe
The splendid beauty, to it we have to ascribe
Its story, we cannot finish it even if millions scribe

Be comfortable, Life is a fort
To keep you in right zone is its purport
Built by you, for your own comfort
To all your enemies you better have a retort

Keep track, Life is a performance
Do best, Keep your head on the cloud
But be firm, fix your foot on the ground
Don't ever get into a trance

Do your business, Life is a stall
Run it on a strong firm wall
Your progress should never stall
You should always stand tall

Face it well, Life is a conflict
Quell all the doubts that it inflict
Deal with it, don't keep a confusion
Be sure to be able to make decision

Understand it, Life is a fingerprint
Observe it, so complex yet so unique
Learn from it, be a better critique
While going leave your best imprint

Be unique, Life is a signature
Know that it's for each his own
Its importance must be known
So, you better know your true nature

Come to terms, Life is a agreement
Between you and the rest
That you would do your best
To stick to it, make all arrangement

Learn to care, Life is a therapy
All it undergoes it deals on its own
All it faces it heals on its own
Learn from its course and be happy

Be firm, Life is a wave
It's difficult to see but easy to feel
You better know how to deal
From your own flight you could save

Get admission, Life is a institute
Enormous subjects, innumerous experts
Tight schedule, pressure exerts
Get to know what all it constitute

Face it delightfully, Life is a circumstance
Pushed at you by other at their stance
But you can make your choice every instance
And prove to the world your true substance

Be mesmerized, Life is a wonder
Take a minute and ponder
You will know its message clear and louder
You are here to enjoy it and feel prouder

Be grateful, Life is a blessing
Befallen on you like a kids kissing
Warm and sweet, nothing missing
Go out to the rain, dance and sing!

Be colorful, Life is a rainbow
Seven different colors mix and make it white
Seven deadly sins without which it's bright
You are the perfect soul, take a bow!

Handle with care, Life is fragile
If it is not held right, it shakes
If it slips out of your hands, it breaks
Keep more care and be more agile

Use it well, Life is a cabbage
Gets weak and rotten as it age
When in prime put to best usage
Don't spoil it to be thrown to garbage

Hold your position, Life is a firing
Be fearless but protected in the battle zone
Seek support and assistance, keep hiring
Face it well and get into comfort zone

Make right choice, Life is a takeaway
Things you take you need to finish anyway
For with you, you cannot take anything away
Know that we are here just to enjoy our stay

Try to uncover, Life is a secret
You will not know it if you just cry
It doesn't reveal it to you unless you try
A questioning mind is one of its secret

Seek its boundaries, Life is a state
You are its ruler, you write its fate
Its reign is under you at any rate
Take charge of it well before your date

Go to its top, Life is a dome
Can grow to a towering height
Carrying on itself a huge weight
Make and take it to a monumental tome

Know it well, Life is a subject
And the subject of all subjects
Covering all, the minute to the mightiest object
Million different possibilities it never rejects

Secure it well, Life is a treasure
It's a boon to you, unlimited measure
Treat equally both pain and pleasure
You will enjoy its worth for sure

Know its reach, Life is a religion
Its absolutely same for every human being
Irrespective of caste, creed or region
Its message for you is to be a better human being

Be prepared, Life is a test
With all your energy do your best
Rewards will sure follow for what you invest
Knowing that, you can peacefully rest

Constant change, Life is a oxymoron
Know its real hidden meaning
Seek to learn, don't be a moron
Only then would you have a meaning

Take the lead, Life is a race
Always be ready to face
Receive everything with grace
In your own way you will be an ace

Don't be disheartened, Life is a crisis
Don't get discouraged, you can get through it
Don't get frightened, you can manage it
To come out, just give your heart more emphasis

Be prepared, Life is uncertain
About that you should be certain
Sometimes, it runs behind a curtain
What's going on behind you try to ascertain

Take its air, Life is a fan
Rotates right when it's switched on
It doesn't care whom the air fall on
You better become its fan

Give your own, Life is a definition
It's all upto you how you want to define
And at all steps you could always refine
By constant pursuit you reach your destination

Feel sacred, Life is holy
If you work honestly and truly
If you don't ever act unruly
You will get to see it wholly

Be in union, Life is a marriage
Of men and women, of opposing poles
Each one having significant multiple roles
And that is how it keeps its own carriage

Read it well, Life is a book
Consists all that you need to know
Contains all that you want to grow
Has everything, have a wider look

Seek the light, Life is a black-hole
Sucks you into it, with a strong pull
You could come out with your strong will
You could win and still be whole

Watch carefully, Life is a lens
Everything looks clean and clear
And you could see far and near
If only you were not under tense

Invest well, Life is a investment
The more you do on yourself, the better
Keep your books very well to the letter
Attain your profits before retirement

Seal the leak, Life is a tap
Closes and opens at your will
Running long, it can fill up the well
Gives you as much as you can tap

Listen to its voice, Life is a telephone
A voice deep within talking on its own
Always with right message in a crystal clear tone
But then the caller is still unknown

Attend it, Life is a concert
Of music and of minds
Savor it joining your kinds
You will enjoy it for cert

Keep going, Life is a walk
Stresses you down, creates pain
All your effort might go in vain
It's not as easy as we talk

Be careful, Life is a bubble
Melts down when in trouble
Be strong, be sure to check double
Don't end up in the rubble

Practice it, Life is a drill
To keep you fit, do it well
To reap the results, do it at your will
You don't get the fruits if you don't till

Keep it fueled, Life is a engine
With courage and confidence as its fuels
You can go as far as you can imagine
Without any struggles, without any duels

Prepare it well, Life is a dish
You could make what you want to savor
Sweet, bitter or sour, whatever flavor
You prepare it, it's all your wish

Know fishing, Life is a pond
With all sorts of big and small fish
Small ones, the big one wants to finish
But then they are not done away in one chance
For the big ones to survive
The small ones must survive
And so they always go in a balance
Know this rule, know this bond

Keep a pace, Life is a walk
With ups and downs, cuts and curves, mud and thorn
It's not as easy as we talk
Distance you reach depends on amount you are worn

Come out to light, Life is a fort
Don't be confined in the name of comfort
Move your ship away from the port
Explore new worlds with all your effort

Bear with it, Life is a turmoil
You have to face it even if your bloods boil
To sow the seeds you need to till the soil
To grow the fruits you have to day and night toil

Live by it, Life is a law
In it there is no flaw
No one is above it, no one can bypass
Know this rule and you are half pass

Be in charge, Life is a disaster
If only you allow it go on its own
Its reign and results you have to own
Take full charge, be its master

Come into its fold, Life is a symphony
To relieve your pain, to relieve your agony
To bring your peace, to bring harmony
That which can't be bought with all your money

Sing it aloud, Life is a song
Learn its lyrics, don't go wrong
Know its tune, be strong
It's melody beautiful and long
Come together and sing along
To its sweetness we all belong

Know it right, Life is a state
It moves from one to the other
It jumps from this to another
You better take charge of its fate

Get adjusted, Life is a loaded-bus
With kids to cremation ready, making full fuss
All matters on earth they all discuss
That is how it is, don't ever cuss

Observe well, Life is a scene
Everything under sun belongs on its screen
Picturesque and perfect, nothing obscene
Draw from it and keep yours clean

Play it well, Life is a gamble
Nothing to gain, you just have to handle
Nothing to lose, but you should not tumble
Whatever your win, you better be humble

Have one, Life is a desire
You will become what you aspire
To reach your place, have the fire
Until you meet your goal, don't retire

Be on stage, Life is a drama
Play your role, know your place
For you no one can replace
Keep rolling your drum, ah?

Live and die, Life is a pair
Opposing sides together, don't despair
For every breakdown there is a repair
Take fresh air and let loose your hair!

Get involved, Life is a monologue
Between yourself there is a dialogue
It is you who sets its prologue
Truth will reign, that's the epilogue

Take good care, Life is a bubble
In the air, all time open for trouble
Just in seconds can end up in rubble
Build a shield, make its strength double

Know the truth, Life is a lie
It's bitter and dry, when the fun of it is removed
But the truth is everyone will one day die
What matters is, when alive, how many you moved

Be amazed, Life is a wonder
How you came, where you go
What it means, why it's so
To know all these, you please ponder

Maintain it well, Life is a engine
Design it right for you are its engineer
Derive optimum performance by being a pioneer
In best state, you can go as far as you can imagine

Believe me, Life is a belief
What you believe is what you get
Believe yourself and have relief
All troubles you can easily forget

Live by it, Life is a principle
Be mindful of what you give into it
For it is what you get out of it
Yes, it's that clear and that simple

Use it right, Life is a pen
Writes all that for which it is driven
Isn't is upto the holder then
What all he writes, how and when?

Reach its top, Life is a terrain
To reach its height, use your brain
You have the inner strength, it doesn't drain
Comes out when you reach for it, just like rain

Quell it, Life is a hunger
For fame, fun and food
For game, glory and good
Eat right and be stronger

Be hooked, Life is a flowing-wind
Thousand thoughts floating in mind
Take care to be keen and kind
That's how you could humanity bind

Be creative, Life is a art
Open up and pour out your heart
Love for all is all that there is
Highest truth, if not, what else is?

Choose the right, Life is a seed
Be careful to sow the right breed
For it can create only its creed
Not for greed, use it for your need

Learn it well, Life is a lesson
For every fruit there is a season
For every root there is a reason
Learn from it and your burdens lessen

Avoid it, Life is a lust
It wants everything, it's a must
Don't heed to it, be just
If you do, you will be dust

Play well, Life is an orchestra
You have to play your music and dance to your tune
For all the external noise you have to be immune
Only then will you be able to go a mile extra

Solve it, Life is a problem
Wherever you see, you can see minus
But you have the power to make it plus
Stick on to it and make it your emblem

Grasp it, Life is a reason
Behind all shades and season
It is behind what is and what has been
It is behind what you see and the unseen

Play carefully, Life is a game of chess
Make meaningful moves, never mess
Take clue from opponents, never miss
You sure will win, God bless!

Know it well, Life is a design
So flawless, with precise perfection
Everything in right place, no exception
Understand it well before you resign

Be on track, Life is a lane
Neat, straight and super-fast
Keep your focus when you move past
While you are in line, there is no bane

Be the priest, Life is a temple
Everyone and everything is God
Worship them all with a clear nod
But following it is not easy and simple

Keep your focus, Life is a track
Speed and attention, have them on your stack
Focus and direction, add them to your rack
All your problems you can easily attack

Be an artist, Life is an art
In its entirety it cannot be thought
With all your money it cannot be bought
But find it, its all there in your heart

Fill it well, Life is a sheet
In the beginning clean and neat
At the end, filled with your act and feat
Make sure to fill it, well before your fleet
Make sure to fill it well, before your fleet

Know its breadth, Life is sky
Which has neither beginning nor an end
You have all freedom to fly high
Every time your limits you better transcend

Be covered, Life is a island
Surrounded by mist and mystery
Connected by trust and history
Use them well to reach your dreamland

Write right, Life is a board
Free at your will to write as you wish
Be in limits and don't go overboard
Keep in check your anger and anguish

Preserve it well, Life is a wine
With age and experience, it gets fine
One should observe and absorb as if its mine
Only then one would over time refine

Carry it well, Life is a burden
For those who know not how to carry it
It's as light as flower for those who know it
You just need to maintain a better garden

Come out of it, Life is a hexagon
Strong and solid like honey combs
Bound in all sides by six severe bombs*
Escape from them and join the band wagon

Look at it, Life is a kaleidoscope
All colors, entire frequency under its scope
Slight change shifts patterns, you try to cope
Its breadth and depth you will understand, I hope

Know the root, Life is a cause
And its effects no one can guess
To know its action, take a pause
I am sure it would really impress

---

*   Six severe bombs – Kama - Lust, Kroda – Anger, Lobha - Greed,
      Moha – Emotional attachment, Mada - Pride, Matsarya – Jealousy

Seek to learn, Life is a language
Often foreign, you know not its age
Its meaning and effect, we can't gauge
Learn it soon and put it to right usage

Create your best, Life is a canvas
Blank in the beginning, brush in the hand
Fill it with all the right that your minds pass
And write the route to where you want to land

Burn it well, Life is a cracker
Bursts well when it has strong inner fire
You will too when you have strong desire
On your wants, keep a tracker

Be in the flow, Life is a river
Friends or foes, floods or drought, you can't foresee
Sometimes clever, sometimes cold, cough and fever
But never stops anywhere until it joins its peaceful sea

Know its shape, Life is a cycle
Of ups and downs, of power and puncture
Of fun and fight, of freedom and fracture
With the bright and right choices recycle

Play right, Life is a gamble
On to the table you bring nothing
When going out, you take nothing
While you are playing, be noble

Catch it right, Life is a boomerang
What goes around comes around
It's your actions it revolves around
Got it? Check again if the bell rang!

Stand tall, Life is a building
It's always under construction, never completely built
Choose right raw materials for your building
Build it to your best, there should not be any guilt

Accept it, Life is a change
Birth to death is its range
The way it needs it will arrange
The working of it is a bit strange

Savor its beauty, Life is a rose-plant
It has both roses and thorn
Separate them, you can't
It is into both that you are born

Water it well, Life is a tree
Its root, it grows with others and thrives
Its fruits, it throws at others and gives
The best of its results, it gives out free

Keep moving, Life is a riding
On a bicycle, to keep balance
You have to keep moving
On the move you are free to dance

Know the sum, Life is a zero
What is given in is taken out
At the end all sums up to zero
With you, nothing is what goes out

Recycle it, Life is a waste
If you don't know its good taste
See it slowly, don't be in haste
You will then enjoy its real taste

Be grounded, Life is a wheel
What goes down will come up
That comes down which was up
You better know its real deal

Pursue it, Life is a quest
To find answers, to find meanings
To find roots, to fly with the wings
You sure will find, don't go unrest

Live carefully, Life is hell
For those who cheat and lies tell
Peace of mind not even for a spell
Bads always ends you up in a well

Live cheerfully, Life is a heaven
For those who are away from deadly sins seven
In its entirety it will be an experience and fun
Believe me, it's true, as true as sun

Hang on to it, Life is a faith
It's so same for all, it's the highest truth
Understand it, don't be like an inexperienced youth
Live to its full, in you have faith

Go find, Life is a desert
Burning sun, hot sand, as your tests basis
With strenuous search, you will find the oasis
Your find you could confidently assert

Know it fully, Life is a tree
For those who seek, it gives an apple free
For those who come, it never denies its shade
Equally to everyone, never considering their grade

See it fully, Life is light
Throwing itself on everyone, equally bright
For those who truly see, it's a grand delight
To see its beauty come out of your night

Be free, Life is a bird
It just wants to fly, to reach sky high
To reach a new horizon, to sharpen its eye
See freedom not just in word

Fight it right, Life is a case
You are the lawyer, you have to find evidence
You have to get verdict, you need to use prudence
Let your case be for a strong cause

Face it well, Life is a trial
It's the toughest of all, there is no denial
Get used to it, leave behind a trail
For the right things you do, you will get a bail

Handle it well, Life is a mess
To be right, to do right, guess less
To see more, to do more, leave your shore
To come out a winner, think and work more

Enjoy it, Life is a treat
You better know how to treat
What you give is what you get
Remember! Only you can make it great!

Know it well, Life is a ploy
Poses you with questions that annoy
Your results depends on the tactic you deploy
Your end depends on the teachings you employ

Be in the flow, Life is a exchange
You give something to get something
Only way by which you change
You only take away what you bring

Come out of it, Life is a obstacle
It's a problem, if you don't know how to tackle
See it from different angle, it works like miracle
With a new view, you sure will come out of shackle

Be in tune, Life is a symphony
The inner voice of it brings in harmony
Listen to it carefully, it's a masterpiece
Enjoy it completely, it is peace

Catch it, Life is a bubble
It contains nothing but is encircled
It contains everything and is circled
Know the truth and be humble

End it well, Spend it well, Life is a pastime
We are here on earth just to have some fun and spend some time
During which many objections and obstacles we will have to
pass
Know that, your destiny can change based on how you your
time pass

Have a great one, Life is a dream
Believe, behave and become, you sure can
Think, speak and act, you sure will attain
Achieving your highest you could joyfully scream

Count yours, Life is a blessing
Don't mourn about what is missing
What you already have start rightly using
You have all the reason to always sing

Capture it well, Life is a flash
Like a lonely star in the night sky
Like the light from a lonely firefly
Comes and goes in a racing dash

Keep running, Life is a marathon
For which there is no beginning no end
Find a new way and keep going on
It's upto you, how far you run, my friend

Be free, Life is a jail
No one can escape out of it
It's never possible to get a bail
Keeps everyone in check under it
It's the rule, you better know it
Your wrong escapades you must curtail
For you never know what it entail
Hence you don't elongate your tail
Be free but be in your limit
So that later you don't have to wail

Keep moving on, Life is a move
Your partner throughout is only love
To make only right moves make a vow
And at the end it will really be a wow

Celebrate it, Life is a ceremony
Be completely involved and enjoy every minute
Be totally engulfed and experience however minute
And thus with yourself and others, always be in harmony

Slow down and savor, Life is a rush
While we are busy in the mad rushing
We are not aware of what we are missing
Take time and slow down, observe and relish

Have a hold, Life is a roller-coaster
Flow with it, at times nothing is as faster
Be with it, at times nothing is as slower
During the entire ride, let happiness shower

Do it well, Life is a work
It is of your lifetime's worth
For right work have right time fork
You will have no worry henceforth

Find your way, Life is a maze
The complexity of which will surely amaze
You have to find your own way out
As a victor you should happily emerge out

Flow with it, Life is a stream
On the surface it's beautifully calm and surprisingly cool
But deep under its violent and is creating whirlpool
While on the move make sure you don't scream

Be curious, Life is a curiosity
About who I am, what I am
About how I am, why I am
Explore it well without animosity

Use it well, Life is a instrument
To exceed yourself of the past
To measure yourself from the past
Utilize it to give the world your best present

Realize it, Life is a delusion
Of Me, mine and other
Of you, yours and another
Come out of it, have a clear vision

Be keen, Life is an observation
Of the observer, of the observed
Of the server, of the served
Of the in, of the out
Of the within, of the without
Observe it all well without any reservation

Be committed, Life is a commitment
Be careful about what you say
Be mindful about what you do
Attain your promise before retirement

Know the reality, Life is a longing
To meet the god, To attain the bliss
To find the fortune, To obtain the peace
Know that to you they are always belonging

Be the change, Life is a change
And that is the only constant
Happening at every instant
Be in the flow, be in its range

Keep flying, Life is a sky
It has no beginning, no end
Its own self it transcend
Keep moving and reach your high

Take it well, Life is a feedback
Any time, whatever you give to it
It's always giving you back
So, think about what you give to it

Keep fighting, Life is a endeavor
Those who struggle hard does it favor
To attain your end, just be braver
Its rightful fruits you could savor

Keep going, Life is a ride
Ups and downs, mountains and valleys by its side
Be in the flow and make it jolly
Enjoy the vision of peaks and nadirs, how lovely!

Sell well, Life is a shop
Know that all are here to sell
Make your best and go hop on hop
That's the one you need to do well

Create big, Life is a company
Of different phases, of different paces
To make it large, to take it places
Always have the right company

Have big one, Life is a view
Of all that's seen and unseen
Of all that's been and unbeen
For everything falls in its purview

Be always on it, Life is a track
Keep focus and keep going whatever the attack
For all the challenges don't ever show your back
And at the end make it a hit musical track

Dare to face it, Life is a turbulence
Always in urgency, like in an ambulance
Face it well and show your endurance
You will be glad of your own emergence

Stay calm, Life is a feat
Though you are on your highest fleet
Savor it with grounded feet
For that's what you need to come out neat

Be in flow, Life is a tide
It sure is not an easy ride
But let courage and confidence be on your side
Chances of emerging out a winner is very wide

Be connected, Life is a network
Utilize it well, achieve your highest work
Invest it on that which is worth
Get as much as your times worth

Defend it well, Life is a case
You are the lawyer, defend it to justice
Between right and wrong choose your cause
All along be truthful to your own conscience

Find solace, Life is a cry
To stand up, to reach the sky
To walk, and to attain high
Reach well before your tears dry

Prepare well, Life is a presentation
Cover everything and make right representation
Present it right for you are its presenter
Finish it well and at end you should not be a resenter

Be competent, Life is a competition
To race, to achieve and to succeed
Take your part, play your role, place your petition
And it's only required of you to yourself exceed

Keep moving, Life is a transition
From a post, from a phase to the other
From a possession, from a place to another
Take charge and make best your position

Keep your cool, Life is a mire
Come out of it however dire
Don't ever put out your fire
Fight till your last breath sire!

Prove it right, Life is a theorem
It has a statement and there is its proof
It has its corollary and also its proof
It has a contrary and also its proof
Know them and know how to follow them

Know it, Life is a philosophy
And it is for each his own
Know yours and make it known
Let that be known in entire geography

Use it well, Life is a day
It has a dawn, it has a dusk
It has the noon, It has the dark
Use all your might to spread the light
Before upon you falls the night

Keep fighting, Life is a struggle
Face it well and come out a winner
Don't hesitate and don't become a sinner
Emerge out as the ruler of the jungle

Build it well, Life is a structure
You are in charge, you are its architect
Make it strong, make it a beautiful architecture
You can build it, and you can make it perfect

Be happy, Life is a pursuit
Of health, happiness and harmony
Of wealth, materials and money
Pursue only those that to you suit

Be awesome, Life is awesome
Try and have a full view of it
Its breadth and beauty, you have to see them
And then be mesmerized by it

Be inspired, Life is a inspiration
Look around and have a feel
All that there is, for sure is real
It only needs your admiration

Find rhythm, Life is random
Million different things happening in tandem
In the midst of this chaos find the freedom
To come to a rhythm, apply your wisdom

Count it right, Life is a countdown
It's on all the time, against you, running up
Pushing you hard and drowning you down
But you need to count well before your time is up

Appreciate it, Life is a chronicle
Every scene in it is serene and a spectacle
Every moment in it is magic and a miracle
Appreciate it thoroughly and allow not to debacle

Contain it well, Life is a quatrain
Pulling itself in all four directions
Continuously moving like in a train
To set it right, take right actions

Compose it well, Life is a poem
Write your own, make sure it means well
Make your own, make sure it rhymes well
See that yours becomes an anthem

Be the best, Life is a test
Prepare well and deliver your best
You must reach your highest
Before you permanently rest

Be cautious, Life is a trap
It doesn't lets you out of its tight grip
By conscious effort, its knots you must unwrap
By emerging out successfully, you could die and RIP

Know your role, Life is a evolution
Taken millions of years to become you
Before you leave create a revolution
Leave behind a sign that you lived too

Be safe, Life is a accident
Without your knowing to you it happened
Everything is important, however happened
Drive through it safely without a dent

Be in the flow, Life is a fall
It flows wherever the forces pull
Take it places, make it beautiful, not dull
Stand tall and make sure you don't fall

Cherish it, Life is a moment
Anything can happen any minute
Everything is significant however minute
Count everything and keep your forward movement

Take part, Life is a contest
All that it throws at you, don't detest
All the wins and losses, you must equally attest
Only then would you have done your best

Sing it well, Life is a sonnet
Covers everything beautifully in one unit
Sees that nothing stays outside, not a single bit
You better know well what all belongs to its net

Know it well, Life is a department
The highest one covering every other
Containing everything like no other
See and know it well before your depart-ment

Study it well, Life is a study
To learn its vastness, always be ready
Acquire it more and make progress steady
Show to the world, you are, how sturdy

Take it well, Life is a turn
Looks like a dead end until we are near
Then suddenly opens up new world, everything so clear
For everything it has given, what do you give in return?

Keep fighting, Life is a fight
For food, for freedom, for fame
For good, for gain, for game
For need, for nothing, for name
Let the side you take be always right

Meet the right, Life is a meeting
Of opinions, of ideas, of minds
Of people, of perspectives, of kinds
Make sure yours was purposeful before ending

Take it easy, Life is a prank
Understand it, have the wit
Don't fret, don't be a crank
To undergo it well you need to be fit

Have it right, Life is a belief
What you believe is what it becomes
What you seek is what that comes
Have right mind set and have relief

Keep counting, Life is a countdown
To the death, to the dead end
Race with it, don't simply bow down
Face it with zest till the end

Know the deal, Life is a compromise
With people, nature and circumstance
But not with your priorities, principles and promise
Only then will your's be an exemplar instance

Be charged, Life is a battery
Once in a while it can go dull
Keep charging it back to full
It's a cycle, know its mystery

Make yours, Life is a list
Of desires and things to have
Of wishes and things to possess
Of aspirations and things to do
Of dreams and things to achieve
See it thoroughly, clear the mist

Savor the sight, Life is a dewdrop
Shining and smiling on a blade of grass
Not knowing its end, in its own class
Enjoy its everlasting beauty before it drop

Have the will, Life is a mill
Of procuring something and producing something
Of one silly thing followed by another sure thing
What you do out of it depends on your drill and will

Mix well, Life is a cocktail
Mixture of juices, some heavy, some moderate, some light
And the harmful ones you must curtail
Know that it makes you sometimes somber and sometimes delight

Work well, Life is a workshop
Work out your best and create your art
Sell it to the bystander's in the world's shop
Show through it to them who thou art

Observe it, Life is a phenomena
Happening always, changing continuously
Covering everything under its arena
Go through it carefully and seriously

Be curious, Life is a suspense
Its secrets, beforehand, it doesn't disclose
You have to endure and explore at your expense
Only then, to its secrets, could you go close

Face it well, Life is a ordeal
Do your best to obtain a good deal
Fight your best to attain your ideal
Emerging a winner, your true self reveal

Come out alive, Life is a den
Containing the dark, the mysterious and the unknown
Housing the cruel, the crooked and the cunning
Know its internals and interiors like a master zen
Keep up your fight and come out winning
Make up your mind and get into the known

Revel at it, Life is a beach
One can sleep on its shore, one can swim on its floor
One has its vast expanse to explore
Do all that you want and can but without any breach

Take control, Life is a yearning
To know more, to see more
To take more, to have more
To get more, to give more
To do more, to be more
To find a balance, you need right learning

Life is like a mountain in the far sight
From here everything looks all right
You don't know how topsy-turvy it might
For climbing till its top you sure have to fight

Life is a dilemma, between life and death
Right from the very first till the last breath
For every breath that you take in is giving life
For every breath that you leave out is taking out life

Take a moment, think a minute or two
What makes you sad and glad too?
Just ask, what your Life and all imply?
Come up with a word and please reply!

Live It Fully. Enjoy!

L ive It Fully, Enjoy! Life is Life!
Create joy for all, spread it, rife

It's all that I have said and a thousand times more
I never could explore to its full core
I never can open its full door
I know I would have gone only till its shore

Do all that you can
Do all that you want
Make your life a wealthy one
Make your life a worthy one

Live your life as much as you can
Get from it all that you want
Make your life a healthy one
Make your life a happy one

Live It Fully. Enjoy! Life is Life!

Part Two

Let there be Light!

This section contains poems on different topics related to life, either directly or indirectly. They are not in any specific order. Each one is independent of the other but all are related to one another through the common string that run through all, that is, Life. I hope that the content impacts the readers Life in a positive way, even if it is a minor change to his daily routine or a major change of his outlook on Life. I hope that there will be Light in everyone's Life.

Let there be Light

Let everyone have insight to see the real beauty
Let everyone have might to do all their duty

Let everyone have a heart of universal love
Let everyone have an art that can, minds, move

Let everyone have the wisdom to differentiate the bad and good
Let everyone always have a gleeful and happy mood

Let everyone have the courage to follow their conscience
Let everyone have the mind to identify superstition and science

Let there be, in everyone's life, many miracles
Let there be, to reach their dreams, no obstacles

Let there be, in everyone's life, a blissful peace
Let there be, in everyone's life, a wonderful grace

Let there be, in everyone's life, an unbounded love
Let there be, in everyone's life, a might to mountains move

Let there be, in everyone's life, bigger dreams and an unlimited drive
Let there be, in everyone's life, an undying energy source to derive

For everyone, let there be light
For everyone, let there be delight
For everyone, let there be bliss
For everyone, let there be peace

Let there be happiness
Let there be kindness
Let there be closeness
Let there be oneness

Let there be justice
Let there be peace

For everyone, let there be light
For everyone, let there be delight

What You Give

B e clear about what you seek, for
What you seek is what you obtain
Seek the right and you sure will attain

Be selective about what you resist, for
What you resist is what persist
Accept the reality and peacefully rest

Be clear about what you focus, for
What you focus is what flourishes
Have focus and fulfill all your wishes

Be sure about what you dream, for
What you dream is what you attain
Dream big and do, and then obtain

Be sure about what you desire, for
What you desire is what you derive
Desire the best, reach out and arrive

Be aware about what you pursue, for
What you pursue is what you procure
Pursue the perfect and be secure

Be sincere about what you aim, for
What you aim is what you reach
Aim for the highest, learn what it teach

Be sure about what you target, for
What you target is what you hit
Target the right and make benefit

Be choosy about what you sow, for
What you sow is what you reap
Sow the right to make a big heap

Be right about what you give, for
What you give is what you get
Give your best to get the best

Be sure about what you practice, for
What you practice is what you pioneer
Practice the right and become a seer

Be perfect about what you do, for
What you do is what you become
Do the right, results you will welcome!

Let the Time Stop

Where are we heading in the mad rush?
What are we thinking to accomplish?
Why we are part of this fools rush?
What are we planning to establish?

What do we want to attain?
What do we want to obtain?
What do we want to retain?
What do we want to maintain?

Who do we want to become?
Where do we want to come?
Who are we deceiving?
What are we receiving?

What do we want to achieve?
What do we want to believe?
Who are we fooling?
What are we pooling?

What are we trying for?
What are we crying for?
Who are we kidding?
What are we bidding?

Who are we trying to betray?
Why are we going astray?
Why are we in a hurry?
Why are we in a worry?

What are we afraid of?
Why are we turned off?
Why do we always get into sore?
Why do we easily get into bore?

Where are we going on ride?
What are we trying to hide?
Do we really know what we are chasing?
Do we really know where we are racing?

Do we really know why we are in this busyness?
Do we really know our real business?
Be sure about what you are actually chasing
Well before you start your mad racing

For you might miss noticing when you pass it
Better yet, you might already be having it
Be sure about what you are actually racing behind?
For there is really no one going your beyond

For there is really no one forcing you from behind
It's only you and your life that you have to cross beyond
Why don't we slow down a bit?
Why can't we cool down a bit?

Why don't we calm down a bit?
Why can't we pace down a bit?
Why don't we relax a bit more?
Why can't we embrace a bit more?

Why don't we explore a bit more?
Why can't we enjoy a bit more?
Take time to think, resist the temptations
Take time to savor, avoid the sensations

Take time to explore, control the impulses
Take time to embrace, reject the reactions
Take time to experience, avert the illusions
Take time to enjoy, decline the delusions

Take time to savor the greenery
Take time to enjoy the scenery
Take time to savor the nature
Take time to enjoy the life

Slow down a bit and contemplate
Cool down a bit and create a template
Calm down a bit and write your fate
Pace down a bit and enjoy your plate!

Don't just jump from hop to hop
Don't make your life a messed up shop
Don't always worry to get into the top
Don't allow your life show become a flop

May you have strong will power
Let your character and strength empower
May you never let your head lower
Let the joy and happiness shower

May you take out your mask
Let the sun shine on your face and you bask
May you get into the real task
Let you have strength to tuff questions ask

May you have some speed breaker
And also some pit stop
May your life never be bleaker
And for you let the time stop!

Make Time

Make time to read to your kid
Make time to feed your kid
Make time to guide your kid
Make time to ride with your kid

Make time to wish good to your kid
Make time to bless bliss to your kid
Make time to teach truth to your kid
Make time to sing songs to your kid

Make time to talk with your kid
Make time to walk with your kid
Make time to play with your kid
Make time to be gay with your kid

Make time to give your kid a warm kiss
Make time to watch him dance, don't ever miss
Make time to listen to his words, what a bliss!
Make time to watch his world, how beautiful this!

Power of Peace and Love

L et power of peace, on earth, strike like thunder
Devastating all human wrong and blunder
That's the one we are all behind, we must ponder
Changes earth, it has all power to do wonder!

Let power of love, on earth, strike like lightening
Removing all hate, all men enlightening
That's the one we are all in need for our lives brightening
Without love, I can't imagine, it's frightening

Peace and love, two wonderful things
Can make miracles to human beings
Peace and love, two powerful things
Can move all human beings

Let there be Peace!
Let there be Love!

Secret of Life

Have you ever heard that sun uses his light to light himself?
Have you ever heard that moon uses his calmness to cool himself?

Have you ever heard, a plant holding its flower for its make?
Have you ever heard air breathing air for its own sake?

Have you seen a river drinking its own water to quench its thirst?
Have you seen a tree eating its own fruit to curb its hunger?

This is the ultimate lesson from nature that we are here just for others
This is the secret of life that we have lived if we have lived for others!

Peace of Mind

Just for a stack of money
 Don't lose your harmony
Just to earn the name and fame
Don't lose your shame

Just to earn the power
Don't your head lower
Just to show your ability
Don't lose your humility

Just to show your earnesty
Don't lose your honesty
Just to go that extra mile
Don't lose your smile

Just to escape a moment's heat
Don't ever resort to cheat
Just to fulfill your unwanted need
Don't ever heed to your greed

Just to show your might
Don't lose your sense of right
Just to prove yourself right
Don't lose your insight

Just to pass your rule
Don't lose your cool
Just because you are in high ranks
Don't forget to say thanks

Just to get an easy ride
Don't lose your self-pride
Just to obtain more prospect
Don't lose your self-respect

Just to attain high success
Don't lose your happiness
Just to fulfill your material hunger
Don't show jealous and anger

Just to gain others control
Don't lose your self-control
Just to reach your goal in a hurry
Don't forget to say sorry

Just to fill up your things cart
Don't lose your soul and heart
Just to win an argument
Don't your head and others torment

Just to attain high net-worth
Don't lose your self-worth
Just to safeguard your guilty
Don't break the unity

Just to escape hardship
Don't lose your friendship
Just to achieve a favorable tie
Don't ever resort to lie

Just to show that you are bright
Don't do that which is not right
Just to get a piece of land
Don't lose your peace of mind!

Roles Rules and Responsibilities

Let us know our roles
Each one has its own purpose
Let us stick to them as poles
Let us perform all that each impose

Let us know our rules
Each one of us has many of them to follow
Let us do anything within what they allow
Let us stick to them and prove our values

Let us know our responsibilities
Each one of us has many to take on
Let us promise to put in as much as we can
Let us perform them all and prove our capabilities

Let us know our roles, rules and responsibilities
Each one of us has many to play
Let us take up all that on our heads lay
Let us do them well and show our abilities!

I have a dream

I have a dream
I need to give it a form
I want to make a reform
I need your support in arm

We need to create a place
Where our kids can live in peace
We need to do that at a faster pace
So that for all of us we could bring solace

Our thoughts should travel, like lighting, faster
The filling words can arrive, like thunder, later
Our actions should result, like spring, desired flowers and fruits
The rest will follow, like winter, with merry conduits

You need to make my dream your dream
Together we should expand our realm
Together we should share the resulting cream
And then we all could happily beam!

I am a Student

I am a student
An humble one at that
Wanting to learn all that
Life wants and hell bent
To teach me
To reach me

I am a student
And I know that I cannot
Learn all that there is thought
Even if I am ready for many a dent

I am a student
And I know that I have my limits
Only for certain areas I have permits
And the rest I can't even rent

I am a student
And I know that I can know only a drop
Of this vast ocean of life, before I drop
Going out for permanent

I am a student
And I know that all I think won't happen
And I know that all I want can't happen
Will work to make happen all that I can, time's every cent

I am a student
With my first cry, I came as a student
With my last breath, I go as a student
All time in between, I will remain a student

I am a student
And I know that I am here on a rent
I try to make best use of time life has lent
I try to pour out all that, in me, latent

I am a student
Of the life, the eternal subject
To study it as much is my object
In its vast scope, I am only a minute object
Will learn and accept the truth and rest reject
With all the energy and enthusiasm inject
This is my goal and I am hell bent

I am a student
Here to learn life, eager and ardent
For that is what I am here sent
I know that it's important and urgent
For I know it won't be back that which has went
For I don't want to miss and later repent
For later I don't want to vent
With anger and resentment

I am a student
Learning every minute as well as I can
Enjoying every minute as much as I can
Experiencing every minute as best as I can
I know it's a loss, every minute that's wastefully spent

I am a student
For me every minute is an enjoyment
Looking at life in new ways with excitement
Adding new view, a bit of enhancement
I know it's for my own betterment
I know I am happy being a student
I want to go on and make it permanent
Will learn and unlearn as much as I am meant
And this will be it, my life's achievement

I am a student
I know that it's very important
Every minute and every moment
For they are foundations for future, distant
With potential to create a movement
And so I will make note and take part in every minute
Observing and collecting all the detail, even minute

I am a student
I know that it's nature's commandment
For Nature is the superintendent
Of every small action and event
Of past, future and present
Of earth's every lady and gent
Who are, will be and went
For me, I think its it's present
To be nature's student
To be Life's student
And I have a no further comment
And Hence, I am a student!

Come out of the Dark

Come out of the dark
Light the divine lamp
With your inner spark
Brighten up the camp

Come out of the shadows
To truly see what life endows
Look far out, out of your small windows
Look high up at sun, you don't see anymore shadows
There is so much to see that the life bestows

Come out of the shackles
Learn from butterfly, how it tackles
Nothing can stop you, there are no obstacles
Once you realize that, you can do miracles

Come out of the ego
It's the darkest of all pits
To your own self that it really hits
Don't hold on to it, please let go

Come out of the shells
Of your rigid view and timid moves
A pearl in the waiting, bring in your spells
You will see an entire world that loves

Come out of the lies
Others you may fool, but yourself you can't belie
Facing the truth is where the actual life lie
If you don't stop, you will soon lose your allies

Come out of the blues
Look at the kids and get some clues
Every day is a new day, with all colors and hues
It's only your response, do you get the clues?

Come out of the hell
Remove the deadly sins seven
Have a dream, create a heaven
Know that you can really do well

Come out of the obstacles
You see them only when you take your eyes off your goals
Know that you can make miracles
Have faith, keep focus, do best and reach your goals

Come out of the mess
Be patient, have a clear vision
Be persevering, reach your mission
Make your confusions less and less

Come out of the past
You can't get back what's already lost
From your today make out the most
Do the best things that forever last

Come out of the future
It turns out only based on your nature
Study your today and good qualities nurture
Without miss you sure will soon mature

Come out of the well
That small one where you dwell
Life is larger than you can tell
Realize that soon and you will do well

Come out of the narrow views
Look out of the horizon, broaden your vision
Add more to it, enhance your mission
For each of your opinions, make regular reviews

Come out of the illusion
Always be in touch with reality
Dream big but don't have delusion
Work till you reach your highest ability

Come out of the delusion
Nothing is yours, nothing is mine
Be grounded and have right vision
And at the end everything will be fine

Come out of the ignorance
Strive to learn and earn knowledge
With humility, your flaws acknowledge
Know that you still have a chance

Come out of the arrogance
The world is not here for you
You are here by the world
Understand it and be in balance

Come out of the trance
Be conscious and follow conscience
Be yourself and trash all nonsense
Always try and take the right stance

Come out of the dark
Light the divine lamp
With your inner spark
Brighten up the camp!

The Two Sons

I gnorance is a deep dark well
As dark as night, just like hell
Knowledge is a deep down spell
As bright as light, I can't even tell

You need to know them both, to know them well
The difference between them is like that between heaven and hell
To make it clear, I have a story to tell
There was a father with two sons who was unwell

He wanted to pass on his properties before he finally rest
He wanted to see if they can protect their nest
He wanted to check their zeal and zest
He wanted to see their urge and quest
He wanted to test who was genius and who was jest
He wanted to know who the right one is to invest
He wanted to pass on the baton to the best
For finding which he thought of conducting a test

He called them both and gave them some paddy seeds
Asked them to store the seeds or do whatever deeds
But he would need them back two years later
He would then decide who was worse and who was better

The ignorant fool thought
That he can get the seeds when he needs
Yeah, he could have easily bought
So he ate them, finished his daily feeds

The knowledgeable one thought for a while
With seeds, decided to do something worthwhile
He went ahead and sowed them in his fields
He watered them and protected them with shields

By the end of two years he had green fields so vast
Full of paddy, grown from all the seeds of previous crops
He had worked hard, pouring his sweat and blood drops
And now he was happy thinking about his toiling past

The day finally came when they all met
The father asked the sons, were they all set
The foolish had bought some seeds which he could easily get
And thought he would win the test, he was even ready to bet

The knowledgeable took his father to his fields
Told him all the pains he had to take
Told him all the gains he could make
Showed him the heap of large paddy yields

The father was happy filled with tears of joy
He knew he had found the true heir for his property in
abundance
He handed the keys over to him, asked him to enjoy!
This, my friends is the difference between knowledge and
ignorance!

One Earth, One Mankind

There is only one earth, one mankind
Let's come together to protect it
Let's work together to preserve it
For there is no other place to go, keep that in mind

On earth we are the highest race
To take its charge, we are the one in place
But we are going elsewhere in a fast pace
Loosing ourselves in a money making race

We are depleting so many resources from her
We are deleting so many rivers that were
We are destructing too many forests that are
We are gradually increasing anger in her

We should be ready to face the consequence
For whatever is done their results will come to pass
It shall be done and there is no escape sequence
And the burden of it, for the next generations, we pass

It's foolish for the parasites to kill their own host, creating
themselves a dearth
We are parasites here, devastating its wealth, our beloved
mother earth
Polluting water, polluting air, polluting nature, plunging
everywhere
Remember friends, Earth is our only refuge! We can go nowhere

Do we not know that earth is the only source?
And sun is the only other precious resource
For our survival, for our sustenance
I always wonder, is it not common sense?

Come together and let us not despair
We still have time, we still have a chance
To set things right, to make the repair
With right set of steps we can always enhance

Consume less, conserve more
Destroy less, preserve more
Waste less, save more
Pollute less, purify more
Trash less, recycle more
Saw less, sow more

Let's work with peace for mankind's glory
Let's kill the violence and no more gory
Let's join our hands and change the earth's story
Let's book a place for us in the books of history

There is no other place to go, let's keep that in mind
Let's come together to protect it
Let's work together to preserve it
There is only one earth, one mankind!

Less - More

Talk less, work more
   Take less, give more
Couch less, walk more
Eat less, do more
Hot drinks less, cool water more
Junk foods less, pink fruits more
Extravagance less, extra care more
Conflict less, concord more
Opposition less, co-operation more
War less, peace more
Hate less, love more
Vice less, virtue more
Foes less, friends more
Words less, work more
Needs less, deeds more
Consume less, conserve more
Destroy less, preserve more
Fear less, hope more
Waste less, save more
Pollute less, purify more
Trash less, recycle more
Say less, do more
Saw less, sow more

If We Can

If we can dream, let us dream heaven on earth
Why shouldn't sweetness of heaven be tasted?
If we can pray, let us pray for the good of mankind
Why should the power of prayer be wasted?

If we can envision, let us vision an enlightened mankind
Why should anyone be left out?
If we can wish, let us wish the best of all for all
Why should anyone be kept out?

If we can do, let us do our best all the time
Why should we need any rest?
If we can say, let's say only the truth
Why should we take any test?

If we can be, let us try to be perfect
Why should we settle for any less?
If we can build, let us build a utopia
Why should there be any mess?

The Song of Happiness

This is the song that was sung
When you were enjoying the happy hour
When you had gone on a long tour
When you saw the blossoming flower
When you reached the success tower

When you were enjoying reading a book
When you busy being a cook
When you had won the war
When you had a toast at bar

When you received your first salary
When you bought that favorite jewelry
When you came out of an old rivalry
When you had that evening of revelry

When you were, to your old friend, writing a letter
When you had fixed a thing and made it better
When you met your favorite hero
When your problems did become zero

When your country won that important match
When your kid caught that very good catch
When you heard your favorite song
When the failure was not your wrong

When a stranger passed on a smile
When you had that lonely walk, a mile
When in a test you came first
When you quenched a long waiting thirst

When someone told you are the best
When you had that peaceful rest
When you had that chance to help
When you were to receive some stranger's help

When you saw your kid's first step
When you received that dearest gift at your door step
When you were drenched in that first monsoon rain
When you erased from your memory all that old pain

When in your garden you saw a colorful butterfly
When you were ready for the first time to fly
When you finished your first writing
When you won that tuff fighting

When you became a proud parent
When you bought a home and stopped paying rent
When you enjoyed that lovely scent
When you gave in your cent percent

This is the song of happiness
This is the song of liveliness
This is the song of joyfulness
This is the song of lifefulness

There are million such songs
That this song cannot contain
Take time to notice and make time to sing
And then happiness obtain
This is the song of happiness!

My Niece, Nature and God

Where is God? Asked my innocent niece
If only I knew the answer, oh, how nice

I would have told her
If only I had known
I would have shown her
If only I had seen
I would have taken her
If only I had been

And then I thought,
And thought
And found out
Is He not there?
Is He not here?
Is He not everywhere?

In the question that she asked
In the rain bringing clouds, just masked
In the innocence that she portrays
In the light from the sunrays

In the breath that she takes
In the big pictures that sky makes
In the breath that she leaves
In the green beautiful leaves

In the glittering eyes from which she could see
In the vast waters of ocean and sea
In her sleek slender nose
In the beautiful red rose

In her abrupt sneeze
In that lovely cool breeze
In her worried, tiresome pants
In the life giving lively plants

In the words that she spoke
In the Mother Nature, perfectly bespoke
In her very quest to know
In that beautiful white snow

In her mind and thought power
In that drizzling rain shower
In her sweet innocent smile
In the longest river Nile

In her heart enclosed in chest cavity
In the wonderful holding force gravity
In her amazingly flexible knees
In the astonishingly big tall trees

In her brilliant white teeth
In the protective atmospheric sheath
In her curious looking sight
In the brilliance of light

In her long tender hand
In the universe, His magical wand
In her angelic looking lips
In the big mountain tips

In her beautiful innocent face
In the eternally vast space
In her genius, so sublime
In the eternally everlasting time

In the atoms that made her, every single one
In the big bright brilliant sun
In the enlightenment she would achieve soon
In the calmness of the cool blue moon

In her cheek with that beauty scars
In those trillion twinkling stars
In her long shining dark hair
In the all-pervading, life giving air

In her keen listening ears
In those sweet juicy pears
In her wonderful touch, so mild
In all those that are in wild

In all her mighty hidden powers
In those many colorful flowers
In her little quests, that she never quits
In all those ripe sweet fruits

In her calm blissful sleep
In the depths of oceans, so deep
In her continued curiosity and wonder
In the big lightning and thunder

In the power hidden in her mind
In the birds, animals and all mankind

Don't I see God in each of these and more?
Don't you see God in each of these and more?
Yes, it's you, me and Mother Nature
That's God and nothing more!

Religion

Hindus celebrate a festival of Muslims in my village
I was born here, oh what a privilege!
Religious harmony is always possible, no it's not a mirage
It's only the so called leaders who are dividing for their own
mileage

Krishna, Jesus and Muhammed were all great men
Revealing to the world the highest wisdom of the mankind
Buddha, Mahavir and Nanak were all great men
Showing to the world the right path to attain the peace of
mankind

That which divides is not a religion
A true religion is one which encompasses all religion
Not specific to any caste, gender, creed, color or region
It's humanity! That's the one and only true religion

Talk truth. Truth is the true religion
Practice peace. Peace is the perfect religion
Serve sincerely. Service is the sacred religion
Be Human. Humanity is the highest religion

Help all men and women in their adversity
Be right and do right, practice integrity
Consider and co-operate, uphold unity in diversity
Reach out to mankind, let our religion be humanity!

My Dear Young Men and Women

My dear young men
My dear young women

You are the bearers of the future
You are the builders of the future
You are the hope of the future
You are the foundation of the future

Wake up and give shape to your life
Wake up and take reins of your life
And the reins of the entire mankind
For you are the lions on the land

Allow not your father to be corrupt
Allow not your acquaintance to be vice
Allow not your elders to be greedy
Allow not your relatives to be jealous

Start your fight for the right
Start your fight right at your home
And let peace be your weapon
And let patience be your power
And let reason be your path
And let truth be your faith

Let that be a sweet fight
Let all of the participants
Fall on to the path of right
Let there be no more awful pants

Read all your history
Know all your history
Learn from its hidden mystery
To make your future
To build a better future
To understand the nature

Open up and realize your potential
You are the storehouse of power
Every right act of yours is essential
Every right act of yours makes better future

What do you want to do in life?
What do you want to be in life?
It's all about doing!
It's all about being!
You are here to do your best
You are here to be your best

Make effective use of your time
Don't waste it when you are in prime
Come out of the idiot shows on the TV
Come out of the idle chats on the internet
Come out of your mundane routine
Don't become a couch potato
Don't just fool around
Don't just sheepishly follow
Finish that which is urgent
Focus on that which is important

Do not mistake
Activity to achievement
Noise to music
Want to need
Busyness to business
Pleasure to purpose
Talk to thought
Entertainment to enjoyment

Follow your own rules
Play your own game
Let right values be your principles
Let truth and peace be your aim

Let your feet be grounded
And let your eyes see the high sky
Let your feet be grounded
And let your soul reach the high sky!

You are the beacon light of the future
Who could spread light, far and wide
You are the torch bearer for the future
Who could spread hope world wide
You are the hope of the future
Who has the hand on the hilt
You are the foundation of the future
On which a utopia could be built

Have faith in your own fight
And don't lose your insight
And don't lose your might
Have faith in yourself than anyone else
That's what matters than anything else

Create a better future for the coming generation
Create a better generation for the coming future
That's what is the aim of every generation
That's what we are here to nurture!

My dear young men and women
You are the builders of the future!

Nothing Matters

Nothing matters
    Yes, nothing matters!
For everyone knows why
Because everything that there is
Came from nothing
And everything that there is
Goes into nothing
That's precisely why
Nothing matters!

We know that it all began from nothing
We know that it all ends in nothing
Anything in between doesn't matter
Everything in between doesn't matter
And so nothing in between matters
And so nothing in between matters!

If I have to sum it all up
It comes only to two words
Nothing matters!
Yes, nothing matters!

The Spring

Spring is telling a wonderful story
While it's restoring the earth's glory

Spring is sweeping its magical wand
On a seemingly sullen barren land
Spring is touching the earth with its mystical hand
And suddenly mother earth's sweet smiles expand!

Trees started growing back to their life
Flowers started blooming all around rife
And on every branch of every tree fruits ripened
Right in front our eyes a miracle happened!

Spring is telling a wonderful story
While it's restoring the earth's glory

Birds start singing new melodious tunes
Leaves start assuming new colorful tones
In a new vigor and vibrancy, the sun brightly shines
To this new magical mystery the mind attunes!

It filled the earth with a new joy
Every sight of it is a beauty to enjoy
It filled the earth with a new hope
That even from a seeming death we could cope

Spring is telling a wonderful story
While it's restoring the earth's glory

That it's possible to look bright even in dearth
That it's possible to smile even while bearing huge weights
That it's possible to come out alive from seeming death
That it's possible to become a phoenix and reach new heights

Embrace the richness of the sweet spring
Let in your heart flow a warm spring
Bouncing back to life like a spring
Welcome with open heart the coming of spring

While it's restoring the earth's glory
Spring is telling a wonderful story!

Lessons from Nature

Feel the nature
Observe the nature
Follow the nature
Be the nature
Earn from the nature
Learn from the nature

Nature is our sweetest mother
About our backgrounds she doesn't bother
Treats all equally as her kids
Favoring any one, she forbids

The rain falls all across
Equally upon the just and the unjust
The sun shines all across
Equally upon the good and the rest

The tree gives out the shade
For the tired and the rested
The earth gives out the aid
For the bestowed and the tested

The fruit tastes the same
For the young and the old
The mountain looks the same
For the timid and the bold

The time runs the same
For the big and the small
The flower smells the same
For the short and the tall

The breeze blows all the same
For the white and the black
The blood flows all the same
For those who have and those who lack

The water tastes the same
For the privileged and the deprived
The sky looks the same
For the loved and the unloved

The spirit is all the same
For the able and the disable
The character is all the same
For the noble and the ignoble

The word means the same
For the read and the unread
The world is the same
For the alive and the dead

The mirror works all the same
For the ugly and the beautiful
The music sounds all the same
For the stingy and the bountiful

The law is all the same
For the fair and the unfair
The beauty is all the same
For the dark and the fair

The smile is all the same
For the virtuous and the wicked
The cry is all the same
For the honest and the crooked

The pain is all the same
For the successful and the failure
The pleasure is all the same
For the sure and the unsure

The joy is all the same
For the weak and the strong
The truth is all the same
For the right and the wrong

The bread is all the same
For the servant and the served
The law is all the same
For the leader and the followed

The values are all the same
For the learned and the unlearned
The rules are all the same
For the educated and the uneducated

The fire is all the same
For the immature and the mature
The sense is all the same
For the vulnerable and the secure

The courage is all the same
For the hero and the villain
The love is all the same
For the daughter and the son

The sleep is all the same
For the affluent and the needy
The sorrow is all the same
For the generous and the greedy

The science is all the same
For the knowledgeable and the ignorant
The conscience is all the same
For the guilty and the innocent

The wisdom is all the same
For the literate and the illiterate
The strength is all the same
For the robust and the delicate

The death is all the same
For the rich and the poor
The breath is all the same
For the pure and the impure

The truth is all the same
For the courageous and the coward
The manner is all the same
For the decent and the untoward

The light is all the same
For the sighted and the blind
The fragrance is all the same
For the grand and the bland

The joke is all the same
For the jovial and the serious
The dignity is all the same
For the common and the famous

The lesson is all the same
For the teacher and the student
The direction is all the same
For the sailor and the saint

The fear is all the same
For the meek and the mighty
The mind is all the same
For the plain and the pretty

The sorrow is all the same
For the fool and the clever
The feeling is all the same
For the worse and the better

The peace is all the same
For the cruel and kind
The life is all the same
For the entire mankind

The nature is all the same
For you, me and every name

Earn from the nature
Learn from the nature!

You

In this complex world, you are a loner
If you don't realize yourself, you will be a loser
In this world so diverse, you are a loner
Go understand the universe; else you will be a loser

It's only you out there
Fighting alone, going nowhere
For you, you have to be there
Escaping this you can't go anywhere

You have to shed the tears
You have to cross the fears
You have to sweat the blood
You have to stop the flood

You have to fight for your right
You have to fight to see the light
You have to fight to stop the fight
You have to fight for the right

You have to wage your war
You have to raise your bar
You have to aim high and far
You have to be above the par

You have to walk your path
You have to do your math
You have to strengthen your faith
You have to face your death

You have to do all the right deeds
You have to satisfy all your needs
You have to walk till the last mile
You have to broaden your smile

You have to play the game
Your wildness you have to tame
You have to face all blame
You have to ward off all shame

You have to fulfill your dream
You have to cross the realm
You have to write your story
You have to gain your glory

You have to quench your thirst
You have to serve yourself first
You have to celebrate your fest
You have to conquer your quest

You have to obtain your rest
You have to do your best
You have to pass all test
You have to keep up your zest

You have to shape your destiny
You have to make your fate
You have to attain high state
You have to make your burdens tiny

You have to achieve your freedom
You have to expand your kingdom
You have to exceed your high
You have to reach the sky

You have to pose your question
You have to find your answers
You have to face the problems
You have to devise the solutions

You have to uphold the truth
You have to unfold your ruth
You have to fight your case
You have to fight for your cause

You have to earn your living
You have to keep achieving
You have to learn your lesson
Your mistakes you have to lessen

You have to save your time
You have to spend your dime
You have to spend your time
You have to save your dime

You have to be practical
You have to be tactical
You have to be passionate
You have to be compassionate

You have to explore the world
You have to enjoy the life
You have to explore your world
You have to enjoy your life

You have to pursue your happiness
You have to quell your sadness
You have to attain your peace
You have to maintain your pace

You have to negotiate your deals
You have to appreciate your meals
You have to clear your loans
You have to suppress your moans

You have to endure your pain
You have to enjoy your gain
You have to enhance your skill
You have to empower your will

You have to accomplish your mission
You have to fulfill your vision
You have to reach your goal
You have to reach your soul

You have to win your battle
You have to earn your title
You have to make your decision
You have to take your action

You have to find your purpose
You have to reach your potential
You have to identify your passion
You have to unearth your compassion

You have to fulfill your hunger
You have to pacify your anger
You have to fight your danger
You have to meet the stranger

You have to enjoy your pleasure
You have to pour out your treasure
You have to harness your talent
You have to show up your potent

You have to realize your Self
You have to ignite the spark
You have to light up the dark
You have to create yourself

You have to find your tranquility
You have to enhance your quality
You have to be your boss
You have to contain your loss

And then at the end of all this, you are not alone
To help you attain all this, the whole world conspires
To help you achieve all this, the whole world inspires
To help you do all this, the whole world comes together
To help you do even more, the whole world plans further
To help you make all this, the whole world motivates you
To help you see all this, the whole world activates you

From its co-operative net, it's not going to leave you alone
In this complex world, you are a loner, yet you are not all alone!

You are the Truth

You are the knower, You are the known
You are the seer, You are the seen
You are the sower, You are the seed
You are the doer, You are the deed

You are the teller, You are the told
You are the seller, You are the sold
You are the seeker, You are the sought
You are the fighter, You are the fought

You are the teacher, You are the taught
You are the catcher, You are the caught
You are the learner, You are the learned
You are the earner, You are the earned

You are the inspiration, You are the inspired
You are the admirer, You are the admired
You are the generator, You are the generated
You are the liberator, You are the liberated

You are the observer, You are the observed
You are the believer, You are the believed
You are the musician, You are the music
You are the composer, You are the composition

You are the singer, You are the song
You are the poet, You are the poem
You are the author, You are the play
You are the writer, You are the written

You are the leader, You are the lead
You are the reader, You are the read
You are the player, You are the gamed
You are the tamer, You are the tamed

You are the sailor, You are the sailed
You are the lover, You are the loved
You are the grower, You are the grown
You are the warden, You are the ward

You are the watcher, You are the watched
You are the manager, You are the managed
You are the guide, You are the guided
You are the mover, You are the moved

You are the heaven, You are the hell
You are the magic, You are the spell
You are the spark, You are the fire
You are the sun, You are the shine

You are the provider, You are the provided
You are the destroyer, You are the destroyed
You are the deceiver, You are the deceived
You are the receiver, You are the received

You are the presenter, You are the present
You are the investor, You are the investment
You are the messenger, You are the message
You are the student, You are the sage

You are the savior, You are the saved
You are the warrior, You are the warred
You are the result, You are the reason
You are the father, You are the son

You are the legacy, You are the heir
You are the past, You are the future

You are the question, You are the answer
You are the beholder, You are the beauty
You are the dreamer, You are the dream

You are the developer, You are the development
You are the enlightener, You are the enlightenment
You are the achiever, You are the achievement

You are the giver, You are the given
You are the driver, You are the driven
You are the rider, You are the ridden

You are the creator, You are the creation
You are the actor, You are the action
You are the director, You are the direction

You are the artist, You are the art
You are the mind, You are the heart
You are the joy, You are the peace
You are the love, You are the bliss

You are the fire, You are the ignite
You are the finite, You are the infinite
You are the origin, You are the original
You are the world, You are the eternal

You are the hope, You are the faith
You are the divine, You are the Truth

The world was born with You
The world moves along with You
The world revolves around You
And the world dies along with You

You are the faith
My friend, You are the truth!

Utopia

What a wonderful place this earth can be
      It's not earth, its heaven on earth may be
If we all wish, as well it will be
If we all will, as well it can be

Not a single lonely man crying
Not a single abandoned man dying
Not a single instance of lying

Its peace everywhere
Its happiness here and there
Its joy everywhere

Not a single fight for wealth
Not a single issue on health
Not a single case of stealth

It's full of fragrant flowers
It's full of splashing showers
It's full of rainbow colors

Not a single instance of pain
Not a single unjustified gain
Not a single event of slain

It's full of cute dancing kids
It's full of laughing newly weds
It's full of lovely singing birds

Not a single man going hungry
Not a single man being angry

It's full of happy homes
It's full of beautiful domes
It's full of fun filled Romes

Not a single word of foul
Not a single wounded soul

It's full of happy men
It's full of happy women
What a blissful omen!
Pray it happens, Amen!

What a marvelous state, compelling!
It's the happiest sun shining
It's the moody moon swelling
It's the mother earth smiling

For all human problems, panacea
That's the state of Utopia!

The Beautiful Rose

Observe that bright beautiful rose
In the morning, when you rose
In your garden where it arose
Out of nowhere, just from moon's dose

It has fought to arrive at this place
But it is keeping a colorful calm face
Though underneath it was a tough race
Its underlying pain you can never trace

It's surrounded by thorns all around
But it's beaming with smile nowhere found
Though it's not going to last long, time bound
The lessons from rose can help you all round

In the morning, when you rose
Observe that bright beautiful rose!

You, Me and Everyone

Different may be our merits and demerit
But same is the spirit we all inherit
Different may be what we eat
But same is how we feel heat
You, me and everyone

Different may be the targets we compete
But same are the tasks we need to complete
Different maybe our monastery
But same are we when in cemetery
You, me and everyone

Different maybe our drinks
But same are we when in brinks
Different may be the things we keep
But same are the reasons we all weep
You, me and everyone

Different may be our taste
But same are we when in haste
Different maybe our costumes and custom
But same is the way we consume and accustom
You, me and everyone

Different maybe our view
But we belong to the same purview
Different maybe what we consume
But same is the responsibility we assume
You, me and everyone

Different may be our heights and weights
But same are our rights and mights
Different may be our looks
But same are our books
Yours, mine and everyone's

Different may be our houses and homes
But same are our examples and epitomes
Different may be the way we talk
But same is the direction of our walk
Yours, mine and everyone's

Different may be our masks
But same are our tasks
Different may be our beauty sense
But same is our common sense
Yours, mine and everyone's

Different may be our measurements
But some are our sentiments
Different may be the way we move
But same is our principle of love
Yours, mine and everyone's

Different may be our currency values
But same are our human values
Different maybe our net worth
But same is our humanity worth
Yours, mine and everyone's

Different maybe our dress and suit
But same are our dreams and pursuit
Different maybe our perspective
But same is our objective
Yours, mine and everyone's

Different maybe our culture
But same is our future
Different maybe our styles
But same are our smiles
Yours, mine and everyone's

Different maybe our deeds
But same are our needs
Different maybe our living ways
But same is where our intention lays
Yours, mine and everyone's

Different may be our nature
But same is our mother nature
Different may be our groups
But same are our hopes
Yours, mine and everyone's

Different maybe our skin color
But same is our valor
Different may be our food
But same is our blood
Yours, mine and everyone's

Different maybe our castes
But we share the same light sun casts
Different may be our race
But we all share the same space
You, me and everyone

Different maybe our looks and hair
But we all breathe the same air
Different maybe the things we explore
But same are the goals we all share
You, me and everyone

Different maybe our place of birth
But we all share same mother earth
Different maybe our religion
But we all belong to the same region
You, me and everyone

Different maybe our creed
But we all belong to same breed
Different maybe our crafts and art
But we are all same at the heart
You, me and everyone

Different maybe the way we live
But we all have the same desire to give
Different maybe our choice
But same is what we all rejoice
You, me and everyone

Different maybe our teams
But same are our realms
Different maybe our goals
But same are our souls
Yours, mine and everyone's

Different may be our languages
But same are our emotional gauges
Different maybe our themes
But same are our dreams
Yours, mine and everyone's

Different maybe our powders and perfume
But same is our inner fire and fumes
Different maybe our products
But same are our conducts
Yours, mine and everyone's

Different maybe our vanity
But same is our humanity
Different maybe our culture
But same is our true nature
Yours, mine and everyone's

Different maybe our prejudice
But same is our justice
Different maybe our kingdom
But same is our freedom
Yours, mine and everyone's

Different maybe our fears
But same are our tears
Different maybe our spices
But same is our species
Yours, mine and everyone's

Different maybe our virtues and vices
But same are our inner voices
Different maybe our tasks and scope
But same are our faith and hope
Yours, mine and everyone's

Different maybe our desire
But same is our inner fire
Different maybe our means and materials
But same are our needs and essentials
Yours, mine and everyone's

Different maybe our share's piece
But same is our inner peace
Different maybe our business
But same is our happiness
Yours, mine and everyone's

Different maybe our solutions
But same are our resolutions
Different maybe our contribution
But same is our evolution
Yours, mine and everyone's

Different maybe our education
But same is our foundation
Different maybe our roles
But same are our rules
Yours, mine and everyone's

Different may be our level, higher and lower
But same are our inner strengths and power
Different maybe our fairs and festival
But same is the means of our survival
Yours, mine and everyone's

Different maybe our flaws
But same are our laws
Different maybe our sports and games
But same are our objectives and aims
Yours, mine and everyone's

Different maybe our dicts and duels
But same are our inner energy fuels
Different maybe our will and wiles
But same is our miles and smiles
Yours, mine and everyone's

Different maybe our lyrics and songs
But same is what our soul longs
Different maybe our vision
But same is our mission
Yours, mine and everyone's

Different may be our answer to violence
But we are all same in peace and silence
Different maybe our pains and pleasures
But same is the joy we all treasure
You, me and everyone

Different maybe our feathers and nest
But same is the way we all rest
Different maybe our pride
But we are all on the same ride
You, me and everyone

Different maybe our butter and bread
But we are all same when we are dead
Different maybe the things we dread
But same is the message we want to spread
You, me and everyone

Different maybe our guilt and sin
But we are all same once in coffin
Different maybe our tricks and technique
But same are we in that, we are all unique
You, me and everyone

Different maybe our music and dance
But same is where we all seek guidance
Different maybe our materials and money
But same are we when in harmony
You, me and everyone

Different maybe our time zone
But we all under same ozone
Different may be the cloths we wear
But same are the burdens we bear
You, me and everyone

Different maybe our means for fun
But we all share the same sun
Different maybe our shame and name
But we are all playing the same game
You, me and everyone

Different maybe what we see
But same is what we all foresee
Different maybe our bikes and car
But same is what we look for in the far
You, me and everyone

Different maybe our modes of pun
But same is the direction we all run
Different maybe our gesture
But same is the way we nurture
You, me and everyone

Different maybe our subjects
But same are our objects
Different maybe the results we get
But same is our target
Yours, mine and everyone's

Different maybe our toys
But same are our joys
Different maybe our games
But same are our aims
Yours, mine and everyone's

Different maybe our plights
But same are our rights
Different maybe our fight
But the same sun is our light
Yours, mine and everyone's

Different maybe our routes
But same are our roots
Different maybe our tasks and routines
But same are our bones and spines
Yours, mine and everyone's

Different maybe the direction of our gun
But all our aim is only one
Different maybe our beauties
But same are our duties
Yours, mine and everyone's

Different maybe our tradition
But same is our ambition
Different maybe our rites and ritual
But same is our friendship, mutual
Yours, mine and everyone's

Different maybe our jeans
But same are our genes
Different maybe our capabilities
But same are our responsibilities
Yours, mine and everyone's

Different maybe the way we speak
But same is our target peak
Different maybe our thoughts
But same are our soughts
Yours, mine and everyone's

Different maybe our stories
But same are our glories
Different maybe our musics
But same are our basics
Yours, mine and everyone's

Different maybe our pass times
But same are our past times
Different maybe our reasons
But same are our seasons
Yours, mine and everyone's

Different maybe our opinion
But same is our dominion
Different maybe our medias
But same are our ideas
Yours, mine and everyone's

Different maybe our beliefs
But same are the reasons for our reliefs
Different maybe our notions
But same are our emotions
Yours, mine and everyone's

Different maybe our wealth
But we all aspire health
Different maybe our cloth
But same is what heart loathe
Yours, mine and everyone's

Different maybe our thing's models
But same are our role models
Different maybe our modes and means
But same are the things our mind leans
Yours, mine and everyone's

Different maybe the things we enjoy
But same is the underlying joy
Different maybe our date
But same is our fate
Yours, mine and everyone's

Different maybe our attire
But same is what we aspire
Different maybe you and me
But yet ultimately same are we
You, me and everyone

What else do you need as proof?
That we are all same and it's not a spoof
Yes, we are all one, it's not a goof
See the truth and don't be aloof

It's the same place we all belong
It's the same things that we all long
Peace, contentment and happiness
Joy, enjoyment and bliss
For You, Me and Everyone!

Quest

Find out your life's real quest
  Then decide upon your steps first
Work on them with earnest
At all times do your best

When you have done your best
You can relax and rest
You sure have passed your test
Results will follow on behest

And then, even if you don't get
All the results that you desired
You need not worry nor regret
For you have done your duty required

Response to the results is always your choice
In whatever you receive you must rejoice!

Duality of Life

Wherever you see, there are two
Look here, we are me and you
It's all the same with life too
Life is a game of one and two

See in its full
Don't be dull
Don't lose cool
Don't become fool

Life is a duel
Life is dual
Life is a duet
Life is a deuce

It is a game of day and night
It is a game of dark and light
It is a game of ladder and snake
It is a game of genuine and fake

It is a game of doubt and faith
It is a game of length and breadth
It is a game of less and more
It is a game of interest and bore

It is a game of blind and sight
It is a game of wrong and right
It is a game of pessimism and optimism
It is a game of cynicism and realism

It is a game of loose and tight
It is a game of dull and bright
It is a game of friendship and fight
It is a game of submissive and might

It is a game of illness and health
It is a game of poverty and wealth
It is a game of fear and hope
It is a game of yes and nope

It is a game of pure and impure
It is a game of rich and poor
It is a game of hide and seek
It is a game of mighty and meek

It is a game of sadness and happiness
It is a game of plus and minus
It is a game of head and tail
It is a game of pass and fail

It is a game of sun and moon
It is a game of curse and boon
It is a game of joy and sorrow
It is a game of today and tomorrow

It is a game of strong and weak
It is a game of ground and peak
It is a game of foolish and wise
It is a game of fall and rise

It is a game of short and tall
It is a game of big and small
It is a game of thick and thin
It is a game of lose and win

It is a game of dusk and dawn
It is a game of known and unknown
It is a game of virtue and vice
It is a game of nasty and nice

It is a game of truth and lie
It is a game of laugh and cry
It is a game of just and unjust
It is a game of trust and mistrust

It is a game of love and hate
It is a game of crooked and straight
It is a game of black and white
It is a game of heavy and light

It is a game of far and near
It is a game of detested and dear
It is a game of real and virtual
It is a game of exclusive and mutual

It is a game of failure and success
It is a game of lack and excess
It is a game of him and her
It is a game of madam and sir

It is a game of lost and found
It is a game of silence and sound
It is a game of earth and sky
It is a game of low and high

It is a game of you and me
It is a game of he and she
It is a game of music and noise
It is a game of disturbance and poise

It is a game of balance and imbalance
It is a game of choice and chance
It is a game of cause and effect
It is a game of correct and incorrect

It is a game of foolish and wise
It is a game of fall and rise
It is a game of likes and dislikes
It is a game of treks and hikes

It is a game of peace and war
It is a game of make and mar
It is a game of tiny and great
It is a game of sour and sweet

It is a game of east and west
It is a game of worst and best
It is a game of empty and full
It is a game of sharp and dull

It is a game of ignorant and learnt
It is a game of gone and current
It is a game of hasty and patient
It is a game of peaceful and violent

It is a game of critic and praise
It is a game of lower and raise
It is a game of lightning and thunder
It is a game of expectation and wonder

It is a game of action and reaction
It is a game of answer and question
It is a game of friend and foe
It is a game of delight and woe

It is a game of ugly and beauty
It is a game of rights and duty
It is a game of roses and thorn
It is a game of night and morn

It is a game of rejection and passion
It is a game of elation and depression
It is a game of problem and solution
It is a game of devolution and evolution

It is a game of construction and destruction
It is a game of consumption and production
It is a game of chaos and law
It is a game of worn and raw

It is a game of multiply and division
It is a game of confusion and vision
It is a game of old and new
It is a game of false and true

It is a game of youth and age
It is a game of calm and rage
It is a game of subordinate and dominant
It is a game of minute and prominent

It is a game of limitation and freedom
It is a game of spring and autumn
It is a game of bottom and top
It is a game of hit and flop

It is a game of guilty and innocent
It is a game of modern and ancient
It is a game of honest and cheat
It is a game of dirty and neat

It is a game of bitter and bland
It is a game of sky and land
It is a game of ignorance and knowledge
It is a game of culprit and judge

It is a game of misery and delight
It is a game of rude and polite
It is a game of luxury and austere
It is a game of complain and cheer

It is a game of dream and fact
It is a game of odd and exact
It is a game of science and art
It is a game of mind and heart

It is a game of reality and imagination
It is a game of station and motion
It is a game of anxiety and tranquility
It is a game of conscience and immorality

It is a game of calm and turbulent
It is a game of past and present
It is a game of past and future
It is a game of man and nature

It is a game of growth and decay
It is a game of predator and prey
It is a game of tamed and wild
It is a game of intense and mild

It is a game of pleasure and pain
It is a game of loss and gain
It is a game of scarce and rife
It is a game of husband and wife

It is a game of natural and artificial
It is a game of genuine and superficial
It is a game of victory and defeat
It is a game of cold and heat

It is a game of God and Devil
It is a game of good and evil
It is a game of abundance and dearth
It is a game of life and death

It is a game of accept and reject
It is a game of subject and object
It is a game of clear and clutter
It is a game of spirit and matter

The list can go on forever
You better notice it now
This is how life will be ever
You better marvel it, how!

All things come together to form life
Dualities bind together to form one
All things fall down to form death
Dualities melt and merge into none!

Heart and Brain

B rain is the store house of information
It is the base for logic and reason
Heart is the store house of love
It is the base for feelings and emotion

It is the heart that helps us cry
It is the brain that helps us try

It is the heart that gives us hope
It is the brain that makes us cope

It is the heart that makes us feel
It is the brain that helps us wheel

It is the heart that helps us heal
It is the brain that helps clinch a deal

It is the heart that gives us energetic zeal
It is the brain that helps differentiate fake and real

It is the heart that gives us energy
It is the brain that brings in synergy

It is the heart that helps us to sympathize
It is the brain that helps us to analyze

It is the heart that helps us not to sink
It is the brain that enables us to think

It is the heart that helps enjoy elevation
It is the brain that helps in calculation

It is the heart that enjoys the season
It is the brain that provides the reason

It is the heart that helps maintain relations
It is the brain that helps establish equations

Brain worries about others gain
Heart rejoices in others gain
Brain thinks about others pain
Heart cries at others pain

Brain ignores others case
Heart acknowledges others case
Brain analyzes others cause
Heart empathizes with others cause

Life is a complex combination
Of the moves of heart and brain
Apply them suitably to situation
Don't let their power drain

Life is a complex mixture
Of the solutions of heart and brain
Use them right according to their texture
Don't miss to use them and don't miss the gain

Life is a complex impulsive
Responses of heart and brain
Utilizing them rightly is compulsive
Yourself you must correctly train

Life is a complex web
Of the answers of heart and brain
Use them to rise and not ebb
Incorrect actions you must refrain

Life is a complex collection
Of the decisions of brain and heart
Use them in the right connection
Better yet learn the art

Both are needed, feelings and reasons
Heart's content and brain's lessons
Both are needed, love and logic
Heart's harmony and brain's magic
One has to know which one to use and when
One's life would be happy and peaceful then!

That Time

How did we arrive at this state?
Why did we force upon us this fate?
How did we create this much hate?

How did we end up creating this classes?
Why did we choose to see the colors?
How did we end up creating the castes?

How did we allow our religions to divide us?
Why did we allow our regions to divide us?
How did we allow our languages to divide us?

I am ashamed by the way
We humans are divided
I am guilty of the way
Many of our actions are guided

I feel bad for being a witness
To all this madness
I cry hard at the foolishness
Of our failing conscience

Don't we know that
The division will lead only to loss?
Don't we know that
The union will always help us amass?

For dividing there are thousand
Different things
But for uniting there is only
One important thing
And that is the first thing
And that is the last thing
That we all are human beings
That we all are human beings

When will be the time when
We all human beings are seen as one
We all human beings are known as one
We all human beings come together as one
I am hoping for that time
I am waiting for that time
I am longing for that time

That will be the most blissful time
In the history of mankind
That will be the most beautiful time
In the journey of mankind
That will be the most memorable time
In the memory of mankind

I am hoping for that time
I am waiting for that time
I am longing for that time!

Mother Earth

D o we know what we are doing?
  Do we really know what we are doing?
Do we know what we are really doing?
We are just exhausting the resources of mother earth
We are just clearing off the treasures of mother earth

We are digging out life from her womb
We are attaching money value to her gift
We are exchanging them for money bomb
And we are exhausting them real fast

We are only reducing her life
We are only killing her each day
And in turn what are we doing?
And in turn what are we really doing?
We are killing our own future generation
We are reducing the future of life
We are cutting down our wombs
Using our own foolish knives
We are building our own tombs
We are digging our own graves

We have become rich
We need to, our lives, enrich
We have become wealthy
We need to become healthy
We have become successful
We need to become mindful
We have become sensible
We need to become responsible
We have become modern
We need to become human

We are in a fit rage
Pursuing the unknown
We are in a mad race
Following the unseen

We just need to calm down
We just need to cool down
We just need to slow down
We just need to go deep down

We need to protect our mother earth
To protect our own progeny
We need to enrich our mother earth
To enhance our own lives
We need to save our mother earth
To save our own selves!

Mother Earth has promised to take care of us till our death
And let us promise to take care of her till our death!

Reclaim Your Life

Forget your past, Cherish your present
Find your cause, Create your future
Write your story, Enjoy your world
Create your history, Leave your legacy
Experience your life, Enjoy your life

Run your race, Obtain your prize
Keep your poise, Maintain your pace
Keep your drive, Remove your failure
Use your might, Achieve your success
Follow your life, Lead your life

Defeat your competition, Defend your stand
Increase your friends, Decrease your enemies
Love your family, Love your friends
Love your neighbors, Love your enemies
Like your life, Love your life

Take your picture, Showcase your skill
Carve your art, Create your masterpiece
Play your music, Sing your song
Shake your legs, Make your moves
Step your dance, Hum your tune
Play your life, Pilot your life

Keep your focus, Keep your calm
Lessen your burden, Reduce your stress
Rejoice your rest, Refresh your mind
Unclutter your space, Save your time
Organize your life, Simplify Your Life

Have your faith, Prove your presence
Clear your doubts, Show your strength
Earn your money, Earn your food
Earn your name, Learn your lessons
Learn your life, Earn your life

Select your food, Increase your health
Exercise your brain, Decrease your pain
Get your sleep, Have your bliss
Have your harmony, Get your Peace
Get your life, Give your life

Kill your evils, Merry your mood
Play your role, Sell your good
Employ your prudence, Enhance your confidence
Satisfy your need, Censor your greed
Satisfy your life, Celebrate your life

Unearth your treasure, Spot your mine
Serve your brethren, Stand your ground
Sharpen your thoughts, Exercise your words
Enrich your taste, Brighten your imagination
Better your life, Brighten your life

Regulate your conduct, Show your zeal
Understand your nature, Attain your perfection
Pour your heart, Care your cadre
Continue your progress, Prove your substance
Prove your life, Improve your life

Kill your anger, Quell your hunger
Quench your thirst, Clear your fear
Fulfill your quest, Pass your test
Relieve your pain, Relieve your agony
Relieve your life, realize your life

Find your place, Reach your destination
Create your tribe, Leave your mark
Show your work, Tell your tale
Do your business, Design your destiny
Do your life, Design your life

Show your mettle, Indulge your play
Decorate your image, Create your fate
Know your limits, Know your worth
Know your position, Know your strength
Show your life, Know your life

Follow your models, Have your morals
Have your values, Hold your principles
Maintain your pace, Follow your conscience
Spend your energy, Keep your calm
Manage your money, Maintain your cool
Maintain your life, Manage your life

Spread your message, Share your dream
Follow your instinct, Choose your path
Heighten your standard, Bolden your glance
Broaden your vision, Strengthen your mission
Study your life, Strengthen your life

Achieve your highest, Reach your best
Achieve your results, Exceed your past
Attain your freedom, Expand your kingdom
Enhance your wisdom, Strengthen your fight
Invest your life, Invigorate your life

Solve your problems, Answer your questions
Correct your mistakes, Catch your misses
Face your problems, Find your solutions
Pose your questions, Give your answers
Choose your response, Provide your meaning
Chase your life, Choose your life

Hold your tongue, Maintain your relations
Refine your manners, Check your attitude
Control your mind, Tame your whims
Watch your moves, Take your charge
Charge your life, Recharge your life

Relieve your pain, believe your faith
Preserve your memories, count your blessings
Live your principles, Value your values
Heal your heart, calm your mind
Define your life, Refine your life

Enhance your smile, Know your strengths
Express your feelings, Embrace your emotions
Chastise your character, Symbolize your style
Reach your challenge, Challenge your reach
Invent your life, Reinvent your life

Find your range, Hit your target
Quell your fear, Clear your jealous
Keep your promise, Keep your cool
Cherish your memories, Relish your moments
Embrace your life, Enhance your life

Read your story, Write your glory
Reach your heights, Retain your name
Choose your books, Select your subjects
Study your surroundings, Save your environment
Read your life, Write your life

Raise your tower, Build your brand
Gain your power, Retain your trend
Build your home, Train your brigade
Raise your head, Reveal your gratitude
Build your life, Rebuild your life

Tell your truth, Bury your lies
Feel your touch, Appreciate your beauty
Uphold your right, Do your duty
Right your act, Act your right
Light your life, Right your life

Power your presence, Empower your sense
Kill your ignorance, Kindle your knowledge
Lessen your unknown, Expand your known
Broaden your view, Enhance your purview
Power your life, Empower your life

Slow your time, Reduce your speed
Manage your timidity, Maintain your humility
Have your modesty, Save your majesty
Save your time, Save your energy
Save your life, Savour your life

Toil your night, Expend your might
Have your plan, Have your ideals
Master your mind, Have your say
Make your decisions, Make your choice
Make your life, Have your life

Increase your depth, Broaden your width
Sharpen your skills, Strengthen your will
Bolden your move, Hold your stance
Believe your self, Express your soul
Broaden your life, Embolden your life

Show your kindness, Create your kind
Recreate your childhood, Replay your memories
Find your solace, Focus your mind
Regret your mistake, Forget your failure
Create your life, Recreate your life

Curb your vices, Realize your potential
Display your virtues, Redeem your sins
Seek your salvation, Achieve your purpose
Realize your self, Enlighten your soul
Lighten your life, Enlighten your life

Discover your passion, uncover your action
Cover your shame, Relinquish your pain
Try your experiments, Trial your case
Satisfy your curiosity, Explore your world
Discover your life, Rediscover your life

Slowdown your time, Keep your schedule
Control your self, Become your self
Control your senses, Curb your vices
Keep your vigor, Show your zeal
Arrange your life, Rearrange your life

Keep your focus, Follow your track
Continue your climb, Reach your top
Move your mountain, Reveal your fountain
Pave your path, Have your hope
Activate your life, Reactive your life

Behold your beauty, Uphold your law
Experience your silence, Quell your violence
Cast your vote, Share your voice
Clear your conflict, Erase your regrets
Assess your life, Reassess your life

Regain your faith, Retain your youth
Rethink your response, Reframe your reaction
Recognize your skills, Understand your capacity
Organize your time, Reorganize your priorities
Rejuvenate your soul, Refresh your senses
Create your life, Transform your life

Sow your seed, Eat your fruit
Strengthen your roots, Lengthen your shoots
Know your caliber, Reach your capacity
Sweeten your smile, Deepen your laugh
Live your life, Relive your life

Rejuvenate your body, Stimulate your mind
Strengthen your will, Fulfill your wish
Stop your cries, Lengthen your laughs
Enable your strengths, Lessen your weakness
Attain your life, Reattain your life

Fulfill your desire, Receive your rewards
Expand your horizon, Reach your goal
Stretch your reach, Deliver your best
Follow your passion, Pursue your dream
Claim your life, Reclaim your life

Dear Mother

Thanks for being that woman
Otherwise I am not sure what
Would have been the fate of man

Thanks for being that woman
Otherwise I am not sure what
Would have been the state of man

You have served your life time
For the betterment of the household
And in that you never had your own time
And in that you were ready to lose your hold

And in that you had lost your identity
And you found your identity in household unity
And in that you had lost your freedom
And you found freedom in your man's freedom
And in that you had lost your joy
And you found joy in your children's joy
And in that you had lost your satisfaction
And you found satisfaction in your man's satisfaction
And in that you had buried your dreams
And you realized dreams in your children's dreams

Just like mother earth
You give out your everything
Just like mother earth
You are patient about everything

Just like mother earth
You pour out your entire self
Just like mother earth
You lose your own self

Yet, just like mother earth
You rejoice in the joys of other
And just like mother earth
All men need you, dear mother!

Your reach is from the smallest hut
To the largest household
And your story is all the same but
Only in different tunes it is told

It is you who has given birth
It is you who has driven earth
I know you are a fighting woman
I know you are the everlasting woman

Forever fighting woman
Forever lighting woman
Forever giving woman
Forever living woman
Forever being woman

Thanks for being that woman
Just like mother earth
All men need you, Dear Mother!
All mankind needs you, Dear Mother!

A thing of Beauty

A thing of beauty is a joy forever
It never goes into oblivion, never
It lives on forever and ever
A thing of beauty is a joy forever

The serene beauty of the rising sun
The beauty when he goes down is even more fun
The shining beauty of the soothing moon
His beauty is really a mankind's boon

The superb beauty of the stretching skies
The patterns, the pictures, their beauty never dies
The striking beauty of the simple flower
The beauty of its color, fragrance and flavor

The structural beauty of the standing tree
Its beauty, breath, branches and bearings are all free
The startling beauty of the staggering universe
The beauty of its dimension, depth and diverse

The breathtaking beauty of the bearing mother earth
For her love, patience and beauty, there is no dearth!
The stunning beauty of the surreal nature
Its force and beauty which can change our nature

The sheer beauty of the never ending time
The beauty of its never missing rhythm and rhyme
The splendid beauty of the ever growing space
The beauty of its vastness, glory and grace

The simple beauty of the innocent child's smile
Its beauty and memory can take you a long mile
The universal beauty of the understanding heart
The beauty of its ability to create and savor great art

The sensing beauty of the savoring mind
The beauty of its vision and imagination of various kind
The seeing beauty of the beholder's eye
The beauty it seeks and attributes for all sights

The encompassing beauty of the glowing light
It's beauty of showing and enabling sight
The embracing beauty of the enchanting sound
Its rhythmic beauty that keeps one astound

The sizzling beauty of the drizzling rain
Its beauty that can make you forget all your pain
The calming beauty of the soothing breeze
It's flowing beauty that makes you at ease

Beauty is in the minutest and the mightiest
Beauty is in the weak and the strongest
Beauty is in the eyes and the sight
Beauty is in the mind and the heart

The most beautiful of all the beauties is the life
It's the beauty of Life with which we can savour all the other beauties
Life endows us with the eyes and the ears to enjoy
Life bestows us with the heart and the mind to savor
Let's make best use of our life and enjoy its beauty
For it's only once we get it, it's now or never!
A thing of beauty is a joy forever!

It's not that which is superficial
It's not that which is artificial
It's not that which goes down
It's not that which dies down
A thing of beauty is a joy forever

It stays on forever, never degrades
It goes on forever, never fades
It moves on forever, never stops
It lives on forever, never dies
A thing of beauty is a joy forever!

(<u>With due respects to Sir John Keats</u>)

Mankind

We have come a long way
But we still have a long way to go
We must keep all our differences at bay
To reach where we all intend to go

We must go together, hand-in-hand
To reach that peaceful dreamland
We must stop all our in-fight
To reach where there is only light

To that heaven on earth
Where there is no dearth
To that land of light
Where there is no single fight
To that home of happiness
Where everyone is in bliss
To that paradise on space
Where there is only peace

We all know where we all stand
Our hearts and souls clearly understand
Our minds must begin to understand

We all know where we need to go
Our hearts and souls are ready to go
Our thoughts must be ready to go

We all know what we need to do
Our hearts and souls are ready to do
Our will must also be ready too!
We have come a long way
But we still have a long way to go!

The LIFE Club

The LIFE club
  It's the best minds hub
It's the humanity's club
The Live It Fully. Enjoy! Club

Come join us, share your story
We are here to enhance humanity's glory
To stop all that's violent and gory
You will be glad you joined, you sure won't be sorry

Come join us, share your time
We are here to bring you to prime
To stop all that's coarse and crime
You will be glad you joined, it's worth every dime

Come join us, share your sorrow
We are here to bear and will borrow
To stop all that's wrong and row
You will be glad you joined, for a better tomorrow

Come join us, share your joy
We are here to expand and enjoy
To stop all that's plot and ploy
You will be glad you joined, I am sure, oh boy!

Come join us, share your dream
We are here to expand our realm
To work towards it and enjoy the resulting cream
You will be glad you joined, with happiness you beam

Come join us, share your tear
We are here to share and bear
To stop all that's unfair and fear
You will be glad you joined, your mind clear

Come join us, share your emotion
We are here to build a strong nation
To stop all that's chaos and commotion
You will be glad you joined, a sure promotion

Come join us, share your dream
We are here to work towards it as a team
To stop all that's cry and scream
You will be glad you joined, you sure will beam

The LIFE club
It's where the brilliant ideas converge
It's where the perfect solutions emerge
It's the best minds hub
It's the humanity's club
The Live It Fully. Enjoy! Club

I Did Not write

No, I did not write all this to impress
For me this is the right way to express
All the thoughts that I didn't want to suppress
What matters to me is the point on your mind it can press

No, I did not write all this for praise
For me this is the right way to rise
I have given words for all that in my mind arise
I would be happy if this could your happiness raise

No, I did not write all this for an award
For me, my life itself is my reward
But then, if this changes atleast one life, it's the real reward
The greatest gift to me that could come forward

For receiving or achieving, I did not write
I wrote because that was the right!

Incomplete

All my poems are incomplete
For nothing ever is complete
And I want you to contemplate
And then you continue and complete
Or disregard and discard

All my poems are my truths
For they are my views and versions of truth
And I want you to consider
And then you respect and accept
Or discredit and reject

All my poems are my truths
They are given to you to find your truths!
All my poems are incomplete
They are left so for you to complete!

The End

Nothing is mine, I own nothing
For when I came on earth, I brought nothing
For when I leave the earth, I take nothing
For its only to mother earth that belongs everything

All that I have written here is only common sense
Nothing mystic neither sixth sense
Tried my best to cut down all non-sense
I hope all this makes to you some sense

All that I have said here is borrowed, nothing is mine
I acknowledge the originators, they are all divine
All this was there already hidden, like in a mine
I just had to carefully look for it and could divine

Keep a copy at home, give a copy to a friend
Keep a copy at office, gift a copy to a colleague
I am not pushing, it's not that I only want to sell
I am just wishing, my little effort will ring a bell!

Don't ever think that I am a poet or a philosopher of life
For what life have I seen so far to be a philosopher of life?
For what have I read or writ to be a poet? Thousands of jewels
yet to see in life
I am just like you and I only hope this can guide and give a
direction to our life

How I thought I should rearrange all these stanzas all by myself
But then I realized, how could I do it? And left it for yourself
For can I ever live and lead your life all by myself?
It's only you who can live your life for yourself

I wanted to remove some, I wanted to defend some more
I wanted to refine some, I wanted to define some more
But as there are downs in life
So there may be flaws in this
As there are the mistakes in life
So there may be errors in this
And hence I have left them all as they are
To suit them all to yourself as you are

I know I have got you confused
But please go back, read and re-read
For am sure, this really is a good mind feed
For am sure, you will find all that you need

For me, the experience of writing this was an elevation
Some new things suddenly coming, just like a revelation
Going back and reading it, I was in astonishment
All this reading and writing, is it an enlightenment?

We are all here to share our art
We are all here to bare our heart
To share with the world, this is what I have
You find out what you have and then give

For every beginning there is an ending
After every ending there is a new beginning
You know not when and where it ends
For everything Life transcends

It's your attitude that your life depend
And your time that how you will spend
Life's calling, go ahead and attend
Thank You very much for reading till THE END!

ACKNOWLEDGEMENTS

Without my parents, my mother Rathnamma and my father Nagaraj, I wouldn't be alive, I wouldn't be what I am today. And there wouldn't be this book in your hands.

I would be eternally thankful and indebted throughout my life to them, for all that they have done to me. Everything in my life including my life is just their blessing.

If there is one person that I miss every single day, even after a decade of his death, it is my grandfather. My grandfather, Kamaiah, was an honest, humble and a hardworking person. It is the fruits of his hard work that I and my family are savoring today. I am thankful to him for all that he has given us.

I am thankful to all my family members without whose support, this book wouldn't have been possible.

I am thankful to all my friends, my teachers, and my colleagues, who have contributed in their own ways to my Life and this book.

Much of the content in this book is inspired by the words, thoughts, and ideas of others, may it be the authors of the books that I have read, may it be many random people that I have come across in my life. I am thankful to each one of them.

Finally You! By holding this book, you are being part of my life. And I am being part of your life. We are sharing our lives through this book.

Without you, this journey, this book, this life wouldn't be complete. I am thankful to you for choosing to be part of my life and to read my version of LIFE.

I wish you Live your Life Fully and Enjoy it thoroughly.
Thank you.

Printed in the United States
By Bookmasters